The MIND at Work and Play

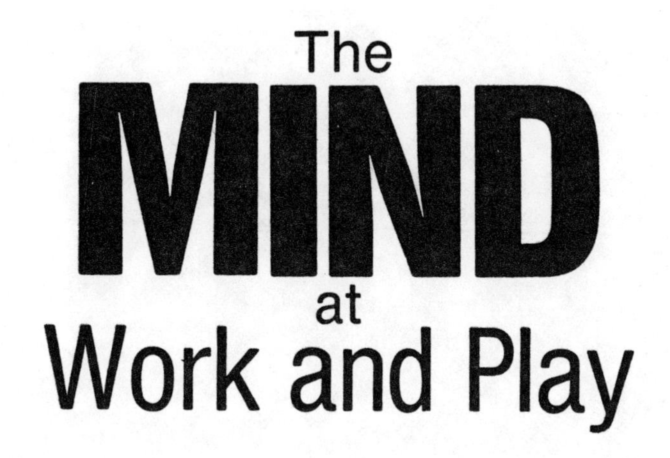

Ronald Englefield

Edited by G. A. Wells and D. R. Oppenheimer

Prometheus Books
700 E. Amherst St., Buffalo, NY 14215

Library of Congress Card Catalog No. 84-42851
ISBN: 0-87975-254-8

Contents

Foreword

During the 1960s the late F. R. H. (Ronald) Englefield committed the fruits of a lifetime of study to paper, in a work entitled "Language and Thought." In it he set out to trace the development of intelligent behavior in animals, beginning with the lowliest of creatures and moving up to the higher primates, including man. A large part of the work was concerned with the probable—one might even say the only conceivable—origin and development of human language. This was followed by a detailed reconstruction of the probable origins and development of the various branches of mathematics.

The manuscript was exceedingly long; and, not surprisingly, since the author's name was practically unknown, it was impossible to find a publisher prepared to print it as it stood. By the time Englefield realized this, his health and eyesight had deteriorated, and he was no longer able to recast the material in a more acceptable form. This task was then undertaken by the two of us, both friends and admirers of the author. First we extracted the section concerned with language, which was published under the title *Language: Its Origin and Its Relation to Thought* (London: Elek/Pemberton, 1977). Sadly, by the time this book appeared the author had been dead for two years.

The present volume contains much of the material remaining in the original work, but in an abridged form. We have regretfully excised passages concerned with the physiology of sensation and the organization of the vertebrate nervous system. We have also omitted some detailed (and copiously illustrated) analyses of the principles of mathematics. On the other hand we have included passages (for instance, on the origins of poetry and the psychology of magic) from other writings by Englefield, not included in "Language and Thought." As we explained in the foreword to the previous volume, our editorial interference has consisted mainly of abridgment and rearrangement. As before, we can assure the reader that although some of the mortar is ours the bricks are Englefield's.

It was Englefield's conviction that knowledge is all of a piece and the means of acquiring it all of a kind. He had no patience with the notion that divine inspiration, mystical revelations, or the like can provide us with anything deserving the designation *knowledge.* Furthermore, as he explains in the concluding chapter of this book, there is no set of self-evident, fundamental truths from which the rest of knowledge can be derived. Along with this view goes the conviction that there is no specific feature of human behavior or human thinking that separates us from the rest of the animal kingdom. However great the differences may appear to be, it is possible to find in other animals forms of behavior that under certain conditions might develop into human culture and, further, to show that such conditions may plausibly be supposed to have existed. In the case of language this point is argued in detail in the earlier book. The present work argues from the same standpoint in regard to the reasoning process, invention, and discovery; the author insists that fundamentally similar mental processes produce, under suitable circumstances, effective behavior, knowledge, and science, and under other circumstances magic and metaphysics. Claims that art, religion, or anything else provides an alternative truth to that discovered by the ordinary processes of observation, reasoning, and experiment are firmly rejected. Also stressed is the importance of play in relation to knowledge—an importance often overlooked when play is regarded exclusively in relation to the psychology of art.

Englefield did not deny that there are many things peculiar to the human species, just as there are to the ostrich or the tuatara. But he held that, if we want to explain these things, we have to look for their relation to something else. The trunk of the elephant, the wing of the bat, the tongue of the anteater are all unlike anything found in other animals. The only way of explaining them consists in comparing them with homologous structures. We can see clearly enough the relation between the hands of a chimpanzee and those of a man. The relation between the thinking of the chimpanzee, as far as it can be inferred from its behavior, and the various spectacular activities of the human mind is no less real for being less obvious.

Some readers may wonder how it is that Englefield makes no reference to the ideas of Karl Popper, whose interests and manner of reasoning overlap with his own. The answer is that Popper's writings had not circulated widely at the time when Englefield was writing. To some extent the two writers are complementary in that Popper writes more from the standpoint of physics and cosmology and Englefield more from that of biology and psychology. They share an impatience with the traditional methods of philosophers. We cannot say with any confidence what Englefield's reaction to Popper would have been, but we do not think that a reading of Popper would have caused Englefield to change his opinions on any important philosophical issue.

We are glad to express our thanks to Mrs. Bärbel Selvarajan for her careful typing of the manuscript.

G. A. Wells
Birkbeck College, London

D. R. Oppenheimer
Trinity College, Oxford

Part I

The Nature of Thinking

1 *Thought in the Evolution of Behavior*

Man is sometimes defined as a rational animal. Many philosophers still appear to believe, with the Scottish philosopher Dugald Stewart (1753-1828), that "it is by the exclusive possession of reason that man is distinguished, in the most essential respects, from the lower animals."[1] But in any biological view of behavior one is bound to recognize that all the essentials of the reasoning process are exhibited in other mammals. The evolution of behavior may be regarded as a gradual progress toward greater appreciation of the real situation in which the animal finds itself. In studying the behavior of any animal, we have to distinguish the *real* from the *sensory* situation, that is to say, the actual state of its environment at any moment from the effect it has on the animal through its sense organs and nervous system. Its life depends on the real situation, but it is the sensory situation that affects its behavior. A shadow cast on a fish may make it dart for cover. The movement is appropriate only because such a change in the incidence of light betokens the proximity of an enemy. Since the connection between shadow and danger is not invariable, such behavior often shows but an imperfect appreciation of the real situation. Let us trace the development of the appreciation of the real situation from its beginnings in the *Protozoa.*

The primitive aquatic creatures that live in a rock pool—for example, the ciliates described by the American zoologist Herbert S. Jennings (1868-1947)[2]—know nothing of the shape, color, or distribution of stones and weeds, or of other living creatures; they react merely to the chemical state or the temperature of the watery medium in their immediate environment, or to the vibrations or radiations (particularly the distribution of light and shadow) that happen to reach them. They are called ciliates from their mode of motion, the greater part of their bodies being covered with very fine, hairlike cilia which, by a beating motion, propel them through the water. The Slipper Animalcule, *Paramecium,* is a typical genus; the common species is about a fifth of a millimeter long and is shaped rather like a cigar. A groove leads back from the front end to form a "mouth" lined with cilia, which have the special function of producing a current of water that carries food in the form of minute plants and animals down the groove. When an individual paramecium encounters some disturbing stimulus (for example, if it swims into water that is too warm), it performs what Jennings calls the "avoiding reaction"; that is, it quickly retreats by the reversal of the ciliary motion, swings round, and then goes forward in a new direction. It is the situation in the immediate vicinity of its own body that determines its behavior and not the circumstances that give rise to that situation. It cannot direct its course *toward* a favorable situation. Although it is sensitive to light as well as to heat, it takes no interest in the source of light or heat but only in the resulting condition at the place where it happens to be. It has no means of knowing that there is a favorable situation a little distance away that is worth making for or an unfavorable one that should be avoided. As long as the situation is neutral, it swims ahead in a spiral course until it finds itself in a suitable place for feeding.

At a slightly higher level than paramecium are ciliates with a somewhat more extensive repertoire of reactions. In these cases it seems that the action taken at any moment is influenced by that which last preceded it. Instead of repeating the same action continually in an unfavorable situation, the animal will change from one item to another in its repertoire, taking more and more drastic measures until the situation is met. For instance, Jennings describes experiments on the Trumpet Animalcule, *Stentor,* which is up to two millimeters in length. If a fine stream of water is directed at it while it is feeding, it will at first contract and then bend its body to one side, as though to avoid the impact of the current. However, if instead of a current of water a stream containing fine particles of carmine is directed at the animal's *disk* (its larger end, furnished with longer cilia than the rest of the body and containing the "mouth"), there is at first no reaction and the particles of carmine are actually ingested as food. Then, as though it objected to the taste, it tries to avoid the incoming stream by bending its body to one side and changing its position.

If this does not have the required effect, the action of the cilia on the disk is reversed so as to cause a current away from the mouth. This drives away the carmine particles but puts an end to feeding and is continued only for a few moments, after which the normal ciliary action is resumed. Further repetition of this stimulus evokes the same reaction for a few times, but if the unfavorable condition continues, then contraction occurs, feeding is stopped, and the mouth withdrawn for half a minute. If on re-extension it is again assailed by the carmine particles, it does not repeat the earlier unsuccessful reactions of bending to one side or reversing the action of the cilia but contracts without more ado. If the stimulus continues, this reaction is repeated, the state of contraction lasting a little longer each time. Finally, however, the animal gives a number of violent contractions in quick succession, breaks away from its attachment, and swims off.

There are three points specially emphasized by Jennings in regard to such behavior. First, in an apparently constant situation the animal's behavior is not constant. Such variations, since they cannot be attributed to external causes, must be due to changes in what he calls the "internal physiological state." In the second place, the number of reactions is small and the effectiveness of a given reaction in the simplest cases depends on the fact that it removes the animal from the region in which stimulation occurs. The action is performed repeatedly until stimulation ceases, or, where the repertoire consists of a number of reactions, these are tried one after another until one succeeds. Jennings calls this the "method of trial." In the third place, there is a tendency in cases where there is more than one available reaction for the one that is successful in removing a stimulus to become, as it were, preferentially linked to it. We shall see that in more complex animals trial behavior, the influence of internal conditions, and the establishment of responses become more evident, but Jennings maintains that they are present in the simplest animals.

The further development of behavior results from the specialization of sensory receptors, the increasing variety of reactions, and the elaboration of a central coordinating system that links particular stimuli to particular responses. When an animal has more or less specialized senses—or at least specially sensitive regions of the body—the effect of a particular stimulus will depend on which part of the body it impinges upon. To a small extent this differential sensibility is found in paramecium, for it is sensitive to contact; but whereas anterior contact evokes the avoiding reaction posterior contact does not. As soon as there is this differential sensibility the animal may react to shapes; for if contact at different points on the body produces different reactions, we may expect to get special reactions to different combinations of contact. If the body is flexible it may be applied to an object so as to obtain the maximum number of points of contact. If there are appendages that are flexible and specially sensitive, these are useful tools for testing the shape of neighboring objects. Local sensitivity to vibrations in the medium permits an animal to determine the direction from which such vibrations are coming.

The development of specialized receptors has another important consequence. By their very nature they enable an animal to react to weak stimuli, "token" stimuli that are not in themselves injurious. Thus light and sound often betoken some other condition that is to be sought or avoided. A dark place is commonly also cool, moist, and safe. In ponds the lightest place is near the water surface, where the gas content of the water may be most favorable, and so on. G. S. Fraenkel and D. L. Gunn have noted: "when there is usually a correlation between light intensity or direction and some important factor in the environment, animals react to light and reap the benefit in relation to that other factor."[3] In other words, it is the real situation that is important, but, as simple animals can know little or nothing about this, they can react only to particular stimuli that it normally produces.

The mere possession of delicate receptors does not fully explain their possessors' reactions to stimuli that affect them. In some way, in the course of evolution, appropriate responses to these token stimuli must have been acquired. In the more highly developed animals such behavior may be learned, but this learning always seems to be based on pre-existing reactions of the same kind. In whatever way we may explain the acquisition of this ability to respond to token stimuli, it is certain that it comes to perform an ever more important role. It constitutes a step toward the appreciation of the real situation, for the objects and situations important to an animal—whether they are favorable or injurious—are generally the source of all kinds of stimulation that in themselves are innocuous. The approaching enemy reflects light, emits an odor, causes air vibrations by its movements—though none of these need have the slightest injurious effect on the intended victim. But all of them are capable of contributing something toward informing the victim of what is coming toward it, and the more information it can gather by means of its specialized receptors the better will be its chance of taking some appropriate avoiding action in time.

So long as an animal has but a restricted repertoire of reactions, it can benefit little from any improvement in its sensory equipment. The ability to discriminate between different environmental situations must be combined with the ability to perform a variety of actions, or no advantage will be derived from it.

There is another aspect of behavior that exhibits a gradual development with advancing evolution. Jennings stresses the *exploratory* nature of the normal activity of paramecium. Since this animal cannot detect at a distance the favorable situations it needs, or infer them from more or less remote signs, its only resource is to keep on the move, changing direction at frequent but irregular intervals, in the hope that sooner or later it will find the situation that suits it. As animals grow more complex in form, more capable of making independent movements with different parts of their body, their modes of exploration can be varied. The concentration of sensory receptors of different kinds—eyes, feelers, chemical and sound receptors—on a movable head facilitates exploration in a bilaterally symmetrical animal that moves rapidly.

In simple animals these exploratory methods may lead only to the discovery of an optimum situation and to an appropriate orientation. But in higher animals, and especially mammals, they may result in an elaborate built-up picture of the environment to which behavior is more or less permanently adapted. Even to the fish, the same rock pool in which paramecium lives is a world full of local features, with a sandy bottom for scavenging, a warm surface for basking, and various cozy hiding places; it knows how to find its way to any part of this familiar territory as its feelings prompt it. This involves reacting to specific objects, not merely to chemical and physical conditions in a medium. The terrestrial mammal has a far more complicated knowledge of its environment and becomes acquainted with many more features of the real world. Since an object presents different aspects when seen from different points of view, such an animal must be able to recognize its various projections as equivalent. (See Chapter 4, p. 31.) This requires an elaborate apparatus in the brain. Often the object must be explored before the animal can identify it; he must walk round it or manipulate it in some way so as to discern a number of different aspects. It is necessary that he should be able to refrain from any reaction until the exploration is complete and then react in a manner that is adapted not to the latest stimulus in the sequence but to the composite effect of them all. This is the essence of memory; it requires something more than a direct connection between sense organ and effector, something analogous to the mechanism of the automatic telephone.

Behavior of this kind may seem very remote from that of paramecium and stentor, and yet there is something in their behavior that may be regarded as the first rudiment of memory. The environmental condition that provokes the avoiding reaction in them does so only if they have been previously adapted to a *different* environmental condition. It is the change from the one to the other that causes this reaction; but this implies that the two conditions can be *compared.* Even in the simplest form of behavior, therefore, the reaction is to a sequence and not to an instantaneous condition. In the higher animals behavior is commonly determined by situations consisting of many phases extended over a long period, each phase exciting a complex sensory pattern.

Another complication arises for the animal that lives in a changing environment, where the reactions that serve the needs of one generation are no longer quite sufficient for the needs of the next. Animals, for example, that live in particular territories in which they have to find their way about cannot, generation after generation, occupy the same piece of country; even if they could the territory would not remain unchanged. Hence it is necessary that every individual should be able to adapt itself to the features of the district in which it happens to be born. Thus we find in all the more highly developed animals some capacity for learning. This means that the connection between the sensory situation and the reaction is not determined in the nervous system from the start but is gradually formed during the early life of the individual.

The development of the brain of the vertebrates has been chiefly concerned with the acquisition of these two powers: on the one hand, the power of adding up a sequence of stimuli into a total effect to which they all contribute; on the other, the power of establishing new nervous connections as a result of experimental behavior. The first power implies the existence of some mode of storage that allows the effect of a sensory situation to be held in suspense for a time until it can cooperate with the effects of subsequent situations. And it is not difficult to see that further development of such a power is associated with the development of memory and imagination. At first only short sequences are retained, and these only for a short time; but the power of establishing new connections in the brain, which is being developed at the same time, makes it possible to preserve the effect of a sensory situation for an indefinite period, so that the memory of past experiences plays a part in determining the reaction to a present situation. We know that in the higher animals behavior is often determined by a combination of memories of very different date, and the same memory may enter into combinations with different associations at different times.

When a large number of such records have been established, the animal's response on any particular occasion will depend on which of its store of memories happen to cooperate with the effects of the current sensory situation. I shall argue in the next chapter that a kind of *internal* trial-and-error behavior then develops, one in which memories of acts and of their effects take the place of the actions and experiences of external experimentation, and that this process of mental experimentation is what we call thinking.

To summarize: With the simplest creatures, a situation must be positively harmful or disturbing to evoke a reaction. At a somewhat higher level we find an ability to respond to token situations, ones that are not in themselves harmful but are signs of a potentially harmful situation. At a still higher level, the behavior of an animal is related not so much to the stimuli that assail it from moment to moment but to the things by which it is surrounded, no matter in what way their presence is conveyed through the sense organs. The senses as a whole are organized so that they afford at least a minimum of relevant information about the real situation; and the nervous system, on the basis of this information, determines behavior appropriate to the real situation. It is, of course, this linkage between sensory and effector organs (such as muscles) that constitutes the crucial part of the machinery of behavior. It must be such as to produce, in response to every common sensory situation, a reaction that causes the animal to behave in such a way that, by anticipating a coming situation, it will evade or exploit it. If we consider the various sense organs and the parts of the brain that receive their input as a mechanism which, by supplying a continuous series of readings and samplings, enables the animal to construct a kind of chart or picture of the surrounding world (so far as it interests him to know it), then it is clear that the progressive efficiency of the mechanism has depended far more on the brain than on the sense organs. As far as acuity, sensitivity, and discrimination are concerned, every one of the human senses is surpassed by those of other animals. It is in the integration of the data received that the human species surpasses them all. This integration depends on the process of building up in the central linking apparatus from a multitude of successive experiences (each one of which provides only a partial, fragmentary aspect of the real world) some kind of lasting representation of that world, so that behavior at each moment may be adapted not to the momentary sensations but to the complex of unperceived events and realities.

Thinking appears to be the latest stage in an evolutionary process that enables the animal to adapt its behavior more and more appropriately to the real situation. Thinking can be a mode of exploration and is as much a form of behavior as looking or listening, sniffing or groping, or any other method of investigating the nature of one's situation. Like other forms of useful behavior this mental exploration comes, in times of leisure, to be practiced for its own sake as a mode of play; from this it becomes adapted for the satisfaction of new needs and acquires functions that are of fateful consequence in the development of human culture.

2 *Experiments on the Ground and Experiments in the Mind*

My argument in this chapter is that the thought processes of the higher vertebrates, including man, are based on what is usually called trial-and-error behavior. Such behavior probably occurs to some extent in all animals and certainly in all that learn from experience. It is the essential preliminary to all habit-formation and consists in a sequence of more or less random acts from which the successful one is selected. The animal, finding itself in a new and unpropitious situation, acts at random and continues to do so until some lucky movement resolves the situation in a favorable manner. This particular action becomes linked to the situation in such a way that, if the situation recurs, the appropriate response is facilitated. The linkage is not always established after the first success, and in animals without a highly developed nervous apparatus many repetitions may be required.

The classical experiments on this type of behavior in mammals are those of the American psychologist E. L. Thorndike (1874-1949), who confined dogs or cats in cages from which escape was possible only if a latch was pressed, a string pulled, or the like.[4] The animal was unfamiliar with the mechanism and could not study it so as to understand its working. It could only bite or scratch or shove at random, hoping that the door would yield. By *at random* I do not, however, mean that the imprisoned animal performed any perfectly irrelevant action, like lying on its back, or any of the peaceful and leisurely operations associated with cleaning or play. There was rather a partial appreciation of the real situation of imprisonment, and the behavior was random only within this frame of reference. By luck, sooner or later, the necessary movement was made, the latch depressed, and the door opened. After a due reward the animal was returned to the cage and allowed to extricate itself in the same way. The operation was repeated until it had learned to open the door without fumbling. The time taken was recorded on each successive occasion and the results graphed.

Here we have the perfect example of trial-and-error behavior, which in man is the normal reaction to an unfamiliar puzzle. There is a popular puzzle that consists of two or more pieces of stiff twisted wire linked together by their loops. The task is to separate them by merely turning and sliding the wires without bending them, until they fall apart. A trained eye may study the geometry of the structure and see how to solve the puzzle before resorting to physical manipulation; but the less sophisticated candidate will resort at once to trial-and-error behavior, wriggling and fidgeting the wires at random until he happens by chance to hit on the correct maneuver.

I have said that thought processes are based on trial-and-error behavior. Now at first it might seem that reflection and planning are the very reverse of random experimentation. In the one case we form a design and act on it; in the other we act without design to see what may happen. But we can form a design and plan our actions ahead only on the basis of past experience. It is because we have already learned how to deal with a number of situations that we can elaborate plans to deal with a new one. New situations are, as a rule, only fresh combinations of elements that we have already experienced in other contexts. If our experience does not include the needed elements for the novel case, we resort to simple trial and error, orientated to the general character of the actual situation. In other words, when we do not know what to do and cannot think out a suitable course of action we just try our luck and hope for the best. If our memory supplies us with the materials for a suitable plan, we work out the correct response before beginning to act; and when we do act, if our reflections have been to the point, we are able to deal with the situation at once without trial and error. In such a case, what is it that happens? What is the nature of this preliminary reflection that makes trial and error unnecessary? It is simply a kind of trial-and-error behavior performed in the imagination. If I need a box to put something in, I do not go around aimlessly on the chance that I may meet one. I visit, in my imagination, the cupboard under the stairs, the shelves outside the kitchen, the coal cellar, the workshop—visualizing each of these in turn in case my memory should tell me whether there is a suitable box in one of these places. And so with more complicated forms of behavior. We first make experimental operations or excursions in the imagination before stirring from our armchair.

For the sake of brevity, I have coined the word *peirasis* as a substitute for the expression *trial-and-error behavior,* and I shall distinguish between *external* and *internal* peirasis. The former is the random experimentation by which animals learn to cope with new situations; the latter is the internal experimentation in the imagination that intervenes between the presentation of a new situation and the animal's response. The German physicist and philosopher Ernst Mach (1838–1916) described internal peirasis many years ago, calling it *thought-experiment (Gedanken-experiment).* He noted:

> Every experimenter, every inventor must have his plan in his head before he can translate it into reality. Although Stephenson knew from experience the coach, the rails, and the steam engine, he must have framed in his mind the idea of a coach driven on rails by a steam engine before he could advance to its realization. No less must Galileo have seen in his imagination the experimental arrangement for the investigation of the falling body before he could in fact set it up.[5]

Mach was chiefly concerned with scientific methods, and his examples are drawn from the history of science. Somewhat later Eugenio Rignano (1870–1930), professor of philosophy in Milan, showed that this mental experimentation plays the essential part in all human reasoning and is also to be found in the thought processes of other animals. According to him, the general principle is that we combine in the imagination a number of experiments, whose separate results we know, in order to discover what the total result will be. The operation may be performed not only in order to solve a current problem but also to ascertain the probability of some future event; or it may be used to establish the facts in connection with a past event. Rignano gives the following example:

> I have lost my umbrella and I am wondering whether by any chance I have left it at one of the places where I had occasion to stop this morning. But I recall that it rained the whole morning; and then I reason thus: it is not possible that I should have come home without my umbrella, otherwise I should have been drenched to the skin, which I was not, since I did not need to change.[6]

The reasoning consists in retracing his steps in his imagination, including the homeward journey through the rain. He can imagine himself making the journey with and without the umbrella, and the result in each case is provided by his memory of many journeys of both kinds. By comparing these results with the present state of affairs he is able to choose one that must in fact be the one that occurred.

As a further example to show that the reasoning process rests on a mental experiment Rignano presents the proposition that there are many people in London who have exactly the same number of hairs on their heads. Since the number of inhabitants of London is greater than the maximum number of hairs a man can have on his head, the conclusion follows. But what is the nature of the reasoning process that leads to this result? Rignano describes it thus:

> I began by imagining the inhabitants of London drawn up in a line, starting with him who had the lowest number of hairs and placing next to him on his left him who had the next higher number, and so on; and I remember that I could see all these individuals drawn up before me in a single line, like so many soldiers whom I was reviewing. . . . Supposing that the first individual had only one hair and that any two persons next to one another differed by never more than one hair, I immediately verified the conclusion that there could not be a place in the line for all the inhabitants of London. . . .[7]

since in that case the population would have exactly equaled the number of hairs on the head of the last man.

No doubt a greater fluency in mathematical calculation would have made this quasi-military operation unnecessary, but though the process might have been abbreviated and would have taken a different form, it would not have been any less experimental in character. The naive process consists in imagining the inhabitants of London arranged in a row in order of pilosity and discovering that if only one were taken from each number group there must be a large number left over. Mathematically the reasoning can be generalized to some such proposition as this: if every one of n individuals possesses one of m characteristics and if $m<n$, then some characteristic must be possessed by more than one individual. But such a generalization can only be reached in the first place by an experimental process, either external or internal, and the application of the general formula requires a mental comparison of the particular with the general case.

Rignano also considers all those trains of reflection that follow such a question as "What would happen if . . .?" The process here is obviously one of imaginary experimentation.

In human behavior, external and internal peirasis are commonly combined; that is, external peirasis is modified by some amount of calculation and reflection, and in planned operations there are always stages where a limited external peirasis has to be resorted to. We draw up our design and make our measurements, but there comes a moment when some particular fitting can be made exact only by a process of trial and error. An appropriate *type* of action is conceived and initiated; but the precise movements must be molded upon the structural peculiarities of the situation, which reveal themselves only in response to actual manipulation.

In all trial-and-error behavior the animal must have some criterion for success. The situation that initiates the behavior must be in some respect unfavorable and need correction, or else favorable and call for exploitation. In the former case the "success" of the reaction will be determined by the removal of some pain, discomfort, or threat; in the latter, by the onset of pleasure, comfort, or promise. In the first case the goal of the peirasis is the removal of an existing situation without regard to what may take its place; in the second case the goal is a particular, desirable situation. With the first are associated pain and fear, with the second pleasure and desire. It is the nature of the pain or the pleasure that determines the general character of the response, but it is the structural details of the actual situation that control the course of external peirasis.

In the lower vertebrates external peirasis, little modified by any kind of mental calculations, forms the normal basis for learned behavior. In the higher vertebrates, and particularly in mammals, processes of thought and deliberation become of ever greater importance. But even in the most complex behavior of men simple external peirasis continues to play an important part. In all scientific investigation both processes continually occur. The scientific experiment is, of course, carefully planned, but ultimately it consists in a resort to trial and error. The difference between the scientific and the naive experiment is that in the former the external peirasis is reduced to a minimum so that the number of trials may be conveniently small. Naive experiments commonly include trials that a little more thought and calculation could have excluded. But of what exactly does this process of internal trial consist? And what, more precisely, is the relation of internal to external peirasis?

The materials for internal peirasis are provided, as I have said, by the results of external peirasis. When a situation has been resolved by external peirasis, the resolving reaction becomes linked to the exciting situation. If there is no internal peirasis the only result is that, when the same exciting situation occurs again, the reaction that was successful on the former occasion will have a certain enhanced facility, a certain tendency to occur more promptly. With each repetition of the situation and its resolution by means of this particular reaction, the latter becomes more and more closely linked to the former, until at length all peirasis is eliminated and the situation has acquired the power of evoking the appropriate response at once. If the brain of the animal provides the resources for internal peirasis, then there is preserved a record of such experiences. Each such experience will consist of three phases: the initial exciting situation, the resolving reaction of the animal, and the new situation resulting from that reaction. And the record in the brain, in whatever way we may imagine it to be formed, will involve three corresponding phases.

Before internal peirasis can be effective, there must be a good store of such three-phase memories; and when a situation has to be resolved by forethought, there must exist either one memory in which the initial phase resembles that presented in the actual situation, or a number of separate memories, whose initial phases will, when combined, yield the equivalent of the actual situation. In the former case the appropriate action will be determined by the particular memory; in the latter it will be composite and consist in some kind of fusion or compromise between the second phases of the various contributory memories. Such composite reactions will usually have to be polished and perfected by a supplementary external peirasis, but the extent to which this is necessary will depend on the number and nature of the memories available.

I have referred to Thorndike's classical experiments on pure external peirasis in dogs and cats, where the animals are unable to bring any relevant experience into play. They cannot calculate or comprehend the geometry of the situation, and they are compelled to grope. When the animal has learned to cope with the situation, it has acquired a new habit. It does not need to have any idea of the mechanism it has learned to operate. When the animal is replaced in its box, it can perform the requisite movement at once, without peirasis, external or internal. If a dog had learned to escape in turn from many such boxes by operating a number of different devices, and if it could remember the actions that were appropriate for each particular device, so that when placed in a new box it could combine previous methods in order to devise one suitable for the new situation, then we should probably be justified in inferring the existence of internal peirasis. That dogs are to a certain extent capable of internal peirasis can, I think, be shown. But it is easier to illustrate the process in its rudimentary form in apes, and for this purpose I shall cite the experiments of the German psychologist W. Köhler (1887-1967).[8]

Köhler placed fruit in or outside the open-air cages of chimpanzees. The fruit was not directly accessible, and various indirect ways—consisting of the use of simple tools, sticks, boxes, ropes, ladders, and the like—had to be employed to reach it. The chief value of the experiments lies not in the mere record of problems resolved but in the exact observation of the demeanor of the apes during the whole course of every experiment. Köhler's description of the animals' behavior is truly admirable. He is concerned to show that the chimpanzee possesses "insight" (*Einsicht*) and that its behavior cannot be accounted for in the same way as that of Thorndike's dogs. But he seems not to understand the relation between external and internal peirasis, and therefore can scarcely appreciate the full significance of his own experiments.

Internal peirasis rests upon the power of forming some internal representation of a situation and of an action related to it when the situation itself is not present and the action is not being performed. It is especially where the animal has learned the use of tools that we may most easily detect its occurrence. We do not see the pictured processes in its mind but only the resulting action. External peirasis, when it occurs, is evident enough, but how can we distinguish an action that follows from internal peirasis from one that is the result of habit or instinct, which occasion responses that are direct and unhesitating like one that has been thought out and deliberately chosen?

The grounds for recognizing the presence of deliberation are briefly as follows: (1) We may know the biography of the animal well enough to know that no habit has been formed of the kind required. (2) In the case of internal peirasis there is a period, which may be long or short but is nearly always appreciable, of apparent quiescence between the presentation of the situation and the effective response. What one observes, then, is a pause in outward behavior and then, without groping or experiment, the appropriate act. (3) The effective situation to which the animal's action is appropriate must comprise some elements not immediately present to it and therefore, since they are essential to the situation, present to its imagination. The last will perhaps seem clearer in the light of specific examples. I quote Köhler:

> On the far side of the bars, out of reach, lies the fruit; on the inside, at the back of the cage, is a sawn-off Ricinus tree whose branches may easily be broken off. To force the tree through the bars is impossible because of its awkward shape, and only a rather large ape would even be able to drag it so far. Sultan is introduced but at first does not observe the fruit and begins to suck one of the branches of the tree, gazing about him with an air of indifference. When his attention is attracted to the fruit, he draws near to the bars, glances through, turns round almost immediately, goes straight up to the tree, seizes a slender branch, wrenches it off, and hurrying back to the bars gets possession of the fruit.[9]

It is apparent that the idea of the tree beside which Sultan had been standing had not yet faded from his memory when he stood at the bars and looked out at the fruit. Combining in his mind the present situation, as presented to his eyes, with the remembered situation of the branched tree, he mentally constructs the solution to his problem and then has only to realize his conception.

On another occasion another of the apes, Koko, is tested; this time the fruit is suspended from the roof.

> At first Koko reaches up with his hand, but in vain. He then looks round him as if seeking something, and suddenly makes for an arbor, three yards from the fruit, climbs up into it to a place where a woody stem stands out conspicuously, but one end of which is held fast in the tangle. He bites it through in two places about ten centimeters apart, climbs quickly down, runs beneath the fruit, but stops without trying to use the little stick which is much too short.[10]

During the whole process of climbing into the arbor and biting off the stem there must remain in the mind of the chimpanzee the notion of the now invisible fruit, for the sake of which the whole operation is being carried out. And when Koko turns away from the hanging fruit in order to go after a stick, he must have in his mind a notion of the stick and of its application to his present problem. With the help of the imagined stick he solves the problem in his imagination and this releases the whole action sequence that takes him from the fruit to the tree and back again. The fact that he underestimates the length of stick required in no way affects the character of his behavior. In Mach's phrase, just as Galileo must have "seen in his imagination the experimental arrangement for the investigation of the falling body before he could in fact set it up," so the chimpanzee must envisage his improvised tool brought into play before he can bring it back to the actual site of operations.

Scores of similar experiments described by Köhler show the same thing. A situation is presented that does not include the means for its own solution. But some recent situation is recorded in the mind, containing elements that, when imported into the actual situation, can provide a solution. If it is still possible to get back into the past situation, then the required elements may be made available, and the present situation solved. In order that such methods may be possible the animal must retain in its mind some record of the past situations from which to obtain materials or clues for the solution of present ones; this is internal peirasis in a simple form. In the more elaborate human peirasis a number of experimental solutions may be tried before one is chosen. In the ape the mental experiment is quickly completed and often put prematurely into action.

Fundamentally, internal peirasis consists in extrapolation from the situation as actually presented. As an animal moves about, it meets in succession many objects and different views and perspectives. If it forgot each aspect as it turned to survey another, it could gain no notion of the solid reality. Yet, if one watches an animal moving in a confined space among obstacles, one may see that, even if it sometimes collides with these, it is obviously conscious not only of those parts of the situation that immediately affect its senses. We may experience the same ourselves. Although we sometimes bump our heads, more often we avoid such accidents even when moving in a confined space. We cannot see what is behind us but we carry the memory of what we have just seen, and the successive views are linked together to form a complete panorama. Such a stereoscopic picture of the environment, freshly constructed and reconstructed as the animal moves about and takes stock of its situation, must be possible to all animals that can move quickly and with agility. No instantaneous view could give the notion of space provided by the continually traversing eye, which sweeps out wide stretches of the landscape, making possible a comprehensive view like a composite air photograph. But for this purpose the views that are procured in succession must somehow be preserved together in the brain so as to function in relation to the animal's behavior as a continuous field.

Let us summarize. External peirasis consists in the performance of a number of alternative actions, more or less at random, until one of them produces a favorable change in the situation. The mental representation of the successful act becomes linked to that of the situation that evoked it and to that of the altered situation that resulted; these newly established ideas so modify the animal's behavior that on another occasion the successful response tends to occur more readily. Internal peirasis is a similar process performed in the imagination with the aid of memory. It is possible only when an adequate stock of experience has been built up by external peirasis. The practical trial consists of three parts: an initial situation, an action, and a new situation brought about by the action. These must all find representation in the mind if the experience is to be available for internal peirasis. The mental representations of these situations and actions are our thoughts and ideas, and the success of internal peirasis depends on their adequacy.

3 *Psychology Without the Mind: Behaviorism*

Some psychologists and philosophers today are afraid to suggest that even human behavior, let alone that of other mammals, can be explained in terms of ideas and imagination, for such terms have been associated with metaphysical disputes. The metaphysical speculations that began with Berkeley, and luxuriated after Kant, so perplexed and entangled the notions of sensation, perception, ideas, reason, emotion, and volition that the whole apparatus seemed to have been discredited. This attitude was further encouraged by the difficulty of making mental phenomena generally accessible.

The Russian physiologist V. Bechterew (1857-1927) believed that science must be based on experiment and observation and that these must be accessible on the same terms to all investigators, so that the findings of one man may be checked and confirmed or corrected by another.[11] But sensations, thoughts, and emotions are not acessible to open observation and experiment, except through their physiological effects. And so he proposed to cease talking about the sensations and emotions of animals and to discuss only their measurable reactions, physical or chemical. He chose to use the term *reflexology* instead of *psychology*. Bechterew's ideas greatly influenced those of his better-known contemporary, I. P. Pavlov (1849-1936). Exported to the United States, reflexology was renamed behaviorism. The zeal of J. B. Watson (1878-1958)[12] and other behaviorist psychologists, however, led them to go further than Bechterew. Not only do they try to confine attention to what is observable in behavior but they even deny the reality of thought and sensation.

Such views are impossible to reconcile with the implications of canine, let alone human behavior. Any dog can play at hide-and-seek. You show him a ball and hide it under a cushion. It has become invisible, but he behaves as if he knew where it was hidden, and adopts the most direct means of recovering it. That he is not necessarily guided by smell is shown by the fact that he may be deceived. If you only pretend to put the ball under the cushion, he will poke his nose there as eagerly as if it were really there. It is as if some kind of image or substitute for the visual sensations had assumed the power to orientate behavior. The peripheral parts of the situation (the furniture in the room) remain unchanged and continue to exert their control over the details of the locomotor or manipulative acts; but in place of the focus of his attention there is now some dummy or mental equivalent that functions in the same way as the focus itself.

We might be tempted to interpret this by saying that the missing elements in the situation are merely restored by association. We know that this is possible and that an animal will often respond to a situation that it has learned to recognize even when, on a particular occasion, significant elements happen to be wanting. But in such a case the response to the defective situation does not differ from the response to the normal one, and if the missing elements are essential the response will give the impression of error and illusion. On the other hand, in the case of the dog looking for the hidden ball there is no appearance of illusion. His behavior is adapted to the new situation. He does not act as if he could see the ball, but rummages under the cushion or tries to pull it out of the way. He appears to have a clear idea of the ball's continued existence even though it no longer is producing any effect on his sensorium. And he localizes this existence quite accurately by a kind of inference from what he observed of the ball's movements before it disappeared. As an orientating stimulus the ball, or some substitute for it, still exists. If you stand in front of your dog, show him the ball, and then throw it away over his head and behind him, he will turn at once and scamper away in the right direction. He has seen it start on its path through the air until it disappeared from his field of view, but his reaction suggests that in his imagination he can follow the path beyond that field, that the real path can be perceived as readily behind his head as in front of his eyes.

Thus the reactions of a dog to a moving object or a changing situation are partly independent of perception. Invisible phases of a familiar process are supplied by some internal operation, with the result that behavior is adapted to the reality rather than to those particular phases that happen to be observed. That this is a fundamental brain function is obvious enough. It is certainly essential to take full account of the facts of physiology and anatomy in any theory of behavior, but this does not mean that such are the only facts or that all our theories must be expressed in physiological or histological terms.

Some philosophers have followed the behaviorists to the extent of being afraid to affirm that a man has a mind. Even the British philosopher Gilbert Ryle (1900-1976) seems to talk their language when he says:

> When we describe people as exercising qualities of mind, we are not referring to occult episodes of which their overt acts and utterances

> are effects; we are referring to those overt acts and utterances themselves.[13]

Ryle uses the word *occult* without explaining it. Probably the old misconception about hypotheses is involved. There was once a textbook of general chemistry, written by a famous German chemist, Wilhelm Ostwald (1853-1932), that went through three editions before its author decided that he was justified in introducing the atomic hypothesis. All the general principles that were required in such a book could be expressed in terms of experimental results; the writer might have summarized his views in words similar to those of Ryle:

> When we describe chemical phenomena as due to molecular changes, we are not referring to occult episodes of which their overt reactions and visible transformations are effects, we are referring to those overt reactions and visible transformations themselves.

But Ostwald thought it more honest to leave the atomic terminology out so long as he could not make use of the atomic idea. Psychologists who follow his example and try to describe human behavior without reference to the mind or its qualities find themselves even more embarrassed than he did. Let us see what Ryle's proposition really amounts to.

We test the temperature of a body by applying our fingers, measuring its expansion, or using a thermometer, and one might claim that the temperature of the body is nothing but the results of such tests. Yet we do, in fact, regard the temperature as independent of them and suppose that they merely serve to inform us about the condition of the body, this condition being independent of us and our curiosity and continuing unaffected even though nobody pays any attention to it. The physicist chooses to think of temperature in terms of vibrating molecules and constructs a hypothetical molecular model by reference to which he explains all the effects of temperature that our various tests reveal. This manner of regarding the matter has proved fertile, since it lends itself to calculations and makes possible predictions that would not be directly inferable from the experimental results. The philosopher may perplex himself with the question as to whether these molecules are real or fictitious, but the scientist is content to know that they are useful.

We may interpret the phenomena of mind in the same way. Ryle seems to suppose that a man's anger is nothing but his angry acts, his grief nothing but his sighs and groans. It is true that the "occult episodes" must ultimately be inferred from overt acts, but this does not make the hypothesis of such occult episodes unnecessary or useless. Although we cannot directly observe an animal's emotions, we say that an emotion is a certain condition that influences its behavior, the latter being in part correlated with its situation, in part with its hereditary makeup, and in part with its momentary emotional or mental condition. The hypothesis of the emotions enables us to generalize usefully and to predict behavior where it would be impossible to establish direct correlations between specific situations and specific acts. Since a man does not always act in the same way in the same external situation, it follows that there is some internal variable, which is a part-determinant of his behavior.

How we describe this internal condition is a matter of scientific convenience. Some kind of hypothesis is indispensable. The hypothesis of states of mind, that is, emotions, purposes, and ideas, serves to link up the chaotic variety of perceptible behavior in the same way that the atomic hypothesis links up the miscellaneous phenomena of chemistry. There may be a number of different ways of determining the constitution of a particular chemical sample, but it is from its supposed constitution that we draw inferences about its probable behavior. It might be possible to draw up a complex table of correlations to show all the specific reactions a given sample would show that had been subjected to any particular combination of tests with such and such results. Each section of the table would have to include hundreds of items, and the application of such a table would require the services of a special computer. The value of the molecular hypothesis and the chemical constitution expressed in terms of it is that the miscellaneous results of chemical analysis can be summarized in a brief formula which, by itself, affords a sufficient basis for predictions about the sample in question. The "occult" structure of the substance is the endpoint or focus of all the various analytical procedures by which the chemist attacks it, and it is the starting point from which all applications have to be calculated. It condenses and codifies all the available knowledge about the substance. And so it is in psychology. The theory of emotions, ideas, and purposes enables us to express succinctly that condition of a man or animal which, in combination with the external circumstances, determines behavior.

The behavior not only of man but also of the Protozoa—and even of nonliving things—cannot be predicted simply from complete knowledge of all environmental conditions. It has to be explained partly in terms of the momentary condition of the behaving thing. The behavior even of a gravitating particle depends at any moment on the gravitational field—that is, its environment—and on its own instantaneous velocity, which is an individual condition inherited from its own private past. Science largely consists in finding suitable hypotheses for a better description and more fertile representation of all kinds of internal states that cannot be directly observed and measured but only inferred from "overt actions." The scruples, therefore, of the philosophers who place an embargo on all hypotheses not only are unnecessary; they are absurd. The suspicious attitude of certain scientists toward hypotheses (Sir Isaac Newton,[14] for example, and Ostwald) is commonly due to a reaction against vain and sterile theories framed in terms of nebulous entities from which no deduction is possible.

4 *The Ideas with Which We Think*

How can we describe the ideas that have to represent reality in internal peirasis? Events and things are presented to us only under particular aspects, and it is the work of the brain to build up the idea of the concrete entity in space and time. We can never *see* a thing except from some particular point of view, but we nevertheless may form a *conception* of it as it exists in three-dimensional space and as it changes over a period of time; this conception is the result of a mental process that links the memories of the various aspects experienced at different times so as to form a complex more completely representing the real thing. All this is so important that I propose to illustrate it before proceeding.

The things to which most of our reactions are related are far too complex to be perceived instantaneously. Objects in space have an indefinite number of aspects, and we have to become familiar with a great many of these before we are acquainted with the thing. Not only does the thing affect our several senses but it also affects the same sense differently according to its position and orientation in relation to our sense organs. A pair of scissors presented to our view may appear, for example, in any one of many forms, but we react in very much the same way to any presented aspect *provided we recognize the thing*. We may say, then, that there exists a whole system of sensory complexes that collectively represent the thing. But only *one* can affect the sensory apparatus at one time. In becoming acquainted with the thing, we learn to connect the separate aspects into a system of memories, and this composite system constitutes our idea of the thing. I use the word *system* rather than *collection* in order to emphasize the fact that the different aspects are linked together in experience not at random but in accordance with their real relation to one another and to the nature of the thing. However different the visual aspects of a pair of scissors may be, they may all pass continuously into each other.

Moreover changes of aspect are related to our own movements. We have learned in the course of dealing with such objects how, by our own action, to change one aspect into another, and the idea we have formed of the thing contains and involves such related activities of our own. One does not know much about scissors if one cannot manipulate them, that is, by one's own movements cause them to assume any of their numerous aspects at will. My sketches show different aspects of the scissors in full view, but we can also recognize them from a mere fraction of a single aspect. They may be partially concealed by another object, yet the visible part may suffice to suggest the whole. Whether it does so will depend on how large a proportion of the whole it is, which part is concealed, how familiar we are with the article, and also what we happen to be thinking about.

The drawings of children and some so-called primitive artists seek to represent not one single aspect of a thing but the thing itself, under no particular aspect, or under a number of mutually exclusive aspects at the same time. It requires a special effort of abstraction to concentrate on a single aspect and reproduce it without admixture. This is especially noticeable with colors. Bright metallic objects are peculiarly difficult to represent in drawings because of the reflections that contribute little or nothing to our idea of the thing. When we first try to represent a piece of bright steel or glass, we are apt to make it a uniform grey or blue or white and overlook the reflections. For these are peculiar to the momentary aspect; they depend on the exact position and orientation of the thing in its actual environment and may never be exactly repeated in our experience.

Many things are recognizable as much by their motion as by their shape or color. The flight of a swallow is at least as characteristic as its form. A motion cannot be represented by any one instantaneous aspect, but only by a sequence. But just as we can recognize a shape from the perception of a characteristic fragment of it, so we can often recognize a motion from a fragment of the sequence. The motion may consist in a change of shape or of place, or both. And there are, of course, many qualitative changes related to the other senses. In all these cases the same formula may be employed: inference from the part to the whole. The whole can never be presented at one time, and our actual experience contains nothing but aspects. The whole can be represented only by that complex system in the mind that is called an idea. To become acquainted with a thing we must study it from many points of view, bring it into relation with other things, handle it, smell it, taste it, and so on; and all this must be done little by little, so that a thorough examination may take a long time.

Apart from this process of linking different aspects of an object, the power to recognize it and separate it from its background involves a further learning process. Not only must the different aspects of the object be associated together but each one of them must be separated from all the various aspects of situations in which they may be presented. The dog, for example, must not only learn to recognize the cat's figure from every point of view; he must also learn to discern each of these projections against many different backgrounds. If the former process is one of synthesis, the latter involves analysis. When we learn to recognize a person or animal by the walk, voice, form, gestures, and so on, this is a case of synthesis. When the bird or the entomologist learns to distinguish the insect from the flower or twig on which it is resting, this involves analysis. In the former case many different experiences must become linked together in relation to a common type of behavior; in the latter a single element must be recognized in many different contexts. In both cases it is the common type of behavior that controls the process. We learn to act in the same way either to a variety of features in the same situation (to different aspects of the same object), or to one common feature in several distinct situations.

For human beings it is so natural to divide what we perceive into separate objects and events—and so difficult to describe any particular situation except in terms of such individual elements—that we are inclined to forget that for many animals these distinct and individual things have no existence and are merged in an unanalyzed background that is only effective as a whole—insofar as it *is* effective. What for a man is a collection of distinct objects, each one of which may be separately attended to, may be for an animal merely a complex situation that must be manipulated and modified until it assumes a shape better adapted to his immediate needs. My dogs will jump on a chair if by doing so they can more easily get at something they want. They are strong enough to push or pull a fairly heavy chair about, and when it is in their way they easily push it on one side. But they do this incidentally in their effort to reach their goal and without paying any attention to the chair. They do not see it as an object to be manipulated and never think of pushing it into a more favorable position where they could make better use of it. It is part of the situation like the floor, the table, the sideboard, or the door. Each of these has its uses and its interest, but it can be exploited only as a fixture, as we regard the trees in a wood or the houses in a street.

The extent to which a man or any other mammal analyzes his situation into components depends on his immediate purpose. For instance, for the purpose of describing the behavior of a certain species of bird, we may say that it builds its nest on the ground. For another purpose we may find it necessary to analyze the nest building into components, and say that the bird first chooses a site, then collects materials, carries them to the nest, and so on. The more minute the analysis, the more complicated will be the description; but if it is carried too far, description of the simplest action soon becomes impossible. The common names available in our languages represent the naive analysis that has been found adequate for normal human needs.

This process of analysis is comparable to the phase of "concentration," which Pavlov described as occurring in conditioning after a preceding phase of "generalization."[15] Generalization is the tendency for a reflex, conditioned in relation to a particular stimulus, to be evoked by a great number of similar stimuli. Thus, a particular note on a whistle, or irritation of a particular region of the skin, however carefully and exactly repeated in the course of the conditioning process, will be spontaneously generalized, so that other notes, or other regions of the skin, so long as they are not too remote from the primary stimulus, become effective in relation to the same reflex. Similarly the young chick will peck at any small object, not only at edible morsels; a very young child may react to all suitably dressed males in the same manner, and he will call them indifferently "Daddy." This, then, is the phase of generalization. But if the animal is rewarded only when the response is made to the correct stimulus, it soon ceases to respond to any other. This is the phase of concentration. In the first phase the animal is more attentive to resemblances and in the second to differences. If the first phase did not occur, that is, if similar situations were not regarded as identical, learning would be almost impossible; for exactly the same situation can scarcely ever be repeated, and so the animal must not be put off by minor variations. He must, however, go on to learn to respond in the same way only to situations that resemble each other in the essential particular, and what this is can be ascertained only by experiment. The first time the situation is presented, the essential feature that calls for the effective response is always accompanied by many others that are indifferent. The animal cannot tell which are more and which are less important until he has tried several times, responding to any complex containing a sufficient number of the features first presented and observing when he is rewarded and when not.

An important factor in the process whereby whole situations are analyzed into components is the distinction between the focus and the periphery of a situation. At first the animal reacts in a generalized way to a complex situation. Then it discovers that the essential feature of the situation is a particular object or group of objects and makes this the focus of its attention, while its behavior nevertheless remains adapted to peripheral details. When my dog, expecting a walk, dances backwards in the comparatively narrow space of the front hall between hatstand, chair, telephone table, aspidistra, and so on, occasionally pirouetting with extreme vigor, I cannot help fearing that she will give her skull a mighty whack against one of the many obstacles. With eyes fixed on me, she seems to pay not the slightest attention to her material surroundings. Yet she has so adequate a spatial consciousness of the structure of the material situation that her muzzle always misses the obstacles by at least an inch. This knowledge has been built up over a long period, and I do not know whether she would not be put out if the furniture were rearranged. At least it is necessary on each particular occasion, before she begins her dance, for her to take her bearings in a brief survey so as to establish her position in relation to the familiar situation. I have the impression that even in an unfamiliar situation she can very quickly construct her picture, or chart, and then operate with fair reliance on her memory.

As a further example, a chameleon stalking a fly seems, at first sight, to act as if the fly were the only significant part of the situation. Yet its advance toward the prey requires that it make use of the physical support offered by surrounding objects. As the creature is usually on a branch and is not able to jump, it must make its way by climbing along the most direct route available; this involves the constant adaptation of its movements to elements in the situation that become significant only when they lie somewhere near the animal's line of advance. The branches and twigs that it grasps form part of the peripheral situation; the fly is the focus. In the absence of the focus the peripheral situation remains without influence on the chameleon's behavior. But when the fly appears it is the peripheral elements, the complex interlacing leaves and branches of the normal environment, which dictate the movements of its hands and the precise line of its advance. Thus the total response is of a generalized nature: the principal orientation is determined by the focus, the particular sequence of acts by the periphery. When the chameleon gets within range its behavior changes. It takes a firm grasp with its hind legs, leans forward in the direction of the fly with its hands curled up in front of its chest, and when it judges the distance to be correct shoots out its tongue, draws in the victim, and proceeds to munch in a final consummatory act that terminates the sequence.

When we compare an animal's relation to its goal with its relation to the peripheral situation, we see the basis of what is usually regarded as a fundamental psychological distinction. Its behavior, as I have said, is oriented toward the goal but is mainly determined in its detail by the remainder of the situation. At different times one and the same general situation may form the background for different goals under the influence of different desires. Whether the chameleon is stalking a fly, seeking water, going in quest of a mate, or merely looking for a sunnier place to bask in, its mode of locomotion remains the same and the general nature of the environment is the same, so that the correspondence between limb movements and suitable foothold is unaffected by a change of goal. The skill it acquires in moving about amongst the foliage and the idea which it builds up of the locality in which it spends its life are impartially employed in the service of all the animal's instinctive needs.

We may say therefore that, in learning how to cope with this complex though constant environment, it acquires a certain knowledge, not only of topography, but also of geometry and mechanics, which it can use for various purposes according to the particular goal and desire of the moment. The smooth twig does not, of itself, elicit a grasping movement in the same way that a butterfly elicits the action of stalking; for until the butterfly appears the twig is nonsignificant. But once the butterfly has attracted the chameleon's attention the twig at once becomes relevant, and the groping hand seems to be drawn toward it as surely and precisely as the whole animal is drawn toward the insect. The difference in its attitude to twig and butterfly is that between knowledge and desire. We say that the attitude to the butterfly is characterized by "appetite," that to the twig and branches that furnish the necessary support for limbs by "knowledge." What we *want,* we strive to obtain; what we *know* we use as a means of getting what we want.

In sum, animals with elaborate and varied sense organs learn to recognize various real situations from many different points of view, and we see the beginning of ideas. The process of synthesis is accompanied by that of analysis, by which whole situations are broken down into components, including a focus. The focus does not remain a particular stable pattern but takes the form of an object with many aspects. Of the further process by which the object itself is analyzed into parts and qualities I shall speak later.

Knowledge is correlated with action. It is what an animal can *do* about the various features of its world that defines its knowledge of them. As it looks around for a method of approach to its goal, each object or part of the situation that it thinks might help creates an impulse to exploit it. The chimpanzee sees a pole, a stepladder, a coil of rope, a stone. Each one of these can suggest a possible operation by which to reach the bananas. A man, even when he has no immediate object in view and merely passively contemplates his surroundings, is nevertheless able to see the house by the roadside, the stream beside the meadow. What he proceeds to do about it—enter the house, sketch it, peer through the window, or knock at the door—will depend on other elements in the situation and his own momentary desires. But his perception prepares him for any of these or similar actions. It informs him how far he must walk to reach the door, how high he must lift his hand to reach the knocker, and what he may expect to happen in response to his knock.

Where the appropriate response is dictated by the situation, where the situation is such as to fire off at once the proper action, perception may be unnecessary. If I sit on a tack I must rise at once. Nothing is gained by first forming an estimate of the length or composition of the tack, or even by speculating whether it could be a pin or a thorn. There may be subsequent reflections, but these are related to a future course of action and have no bearing on my immediate response, which is completed before they can begin. But if I see the tack on the chair before I sit down, the case is different. I am not at once impelled by such a sight to any particular action; I merely feel myself prepared. Whatever action I may be contemplating is apt to be modified by this fuller appreciation of the finer details of my environment. I know that if I am to sit I must first remove the tack or sit elsewhere. If I see somebody else approach the chair I am again fully equipped to deal with such a situation, whether I choose the course of charity or of malice. In short I feel myself master of the situation as far as that tack is concerned. I can only see a little bright point set off against the dull brown seat, but I perceive not only that tiny glint of light but all the possibilities of such a situation and all the appropriate actions I might usefully take in relation to it. None of the actions may be actually performed. But even without visualizing them, which in any case I could only do one by one somewhat slowly, I know that they are available, I feel sure of myself, and this confidence is sometimes all that can be discovered in my mind when I try to identify the perceptual process. When I contemplate the situation at length and at leisure I may review all the possible courses of action on which I might embark and speculate on all the probable consequences. But if the situation is familiar I dispense with such a review, for I am confident that I shall not be at a loss. This seems to be the essential relation between reflection and perception.

The degree of perception is proportional to the multitude of ways in which an animal can exploit a particular situation. Unless it has limbs that are capable of many and diverse movements it cannot exploit many of the features of its environment. The horse's hoofs are capable of little beside their primary function of locomotion. The forepaws of the cat have many more potentialities. The hands of the ape are as much superior to the paws of the cat in the variety of possible applications as the latter are to the horse's hoofs. Capacity for varied manipulation of the environment is partly dependent on skeletal and muscular structure and partly on the nervous mechanism that underlies and informs this structure, but the two evolve together, continually reacting one upon the other. The human hand was as indispensable for the development of human capacity as the human brain. Swift's Houyhnhnm is a physiological absurdity.

If every view we obtain of the object in the course of our examination, every perception of it, every observation of its behavior under this or that condition is duly recorded in our memory, it is plain that when we subsequently think of the object any or all of these memories may be revived. But they can be revived only in succession, just as the perceptions were only to be had in succession. Hence, when a man speaks of an idea suddenly coming into his mind, either it must be an exceedingly fragmentary or flimsy idea or he means that some element of the idea has presented itself and he assumes that the rest will follow in time. An idea can never fully represent an object or a situation or an event; when we speak of two or more persons having the same idea we can only mean that they have similar ideas. Insofar as two persons do have approximately the same idea it must be because they have derived it from a similar set of experiences. Because they give the same name to a thing, it is not to be assumed that their ideas of it necessarily have much in common.

In internal peirasis the whole cluster of related memories that represent the aspects and phases of an object, situation, or event cannot be utilized. Something less must suffice. When we have thought out some little problem successfully and put the conclusion into effect, we do not in recollection realize how little of the real situation was represented in our reflections. A man is thinking out a plan for repairing his greenhouse and recalls that he is short of nails and needs a pane of glass. He decides to run down to the hardware store immediately after lunch, but then he remembers that it is an early closing day. That means that he must start at once, and since it is already late he must go on his bicycle. But that reminds him that he has a flat tire and will have to borrow his wife's machine. And so on. This and much more may pass through his mind in a short time, and it is certain that the various "ideas" that are involved must be represented in a very perfunctory way. All the elements in such a train of thought and all the transitions from condition to consequence are so familiar and habitual that each configuration dissolves into the next even before it has been fully formed. When this wont and familiarity are lacking, the process slows down and in the imagination one seems to linger around each idea as it arises and survey it from a number of points of view, calling up in succession many aspects of the entire complex relevant to the present need.

Consider, for instance, what happens in our minds when we stand in the empty rooms of our new house and try to decide how our furniture will fit into them. Shall we put the piano here or there? In our imagination we try it first in the one place, then in the other. But for this purpose we do not need to picture the laborious process of moving it about nor the muscular efforts entailed. Looking at a doorway we suddenly think that the chest of drawers will never go through it. A thousand other familiar aspects of the chest remain latent and will be revived only if and when they are relevant. We take for granted everything that is not actually in question. In considering whether to paint a cupboard white or green, we do not need to picture ourselves handling the brush. It is only by this strict economy of thought that we can make any mental experiments. The more objects we have to bring together in our experiment and the more complex the situation we have to construct, the more sparing we must be with the representative ideas or images with which we think.

In describing such trains of thought one may speak of the "idea" of the greenhouse, the bicycle, or the piano, but this idea, according to circumstances, may merely represent the sound of a word or it may consist of a whole system of memories gathered during a lifetime. "Early closing day" is a complex set of activities affecting the behavior of a large section of the population; to form an exhaustive idea of the whole operation would be far beyond the capacity of any mind. But so far as it affects the man who wants some nails, it merely amounts to an inhibitory effect on any impulse to go and buy some. The idea of a greenhouse may be highly complex and require a long and sustained effort of the memory and imagination for anything like a reconstitution of it in the mind; but for the purpose of such a brief deliberation the fleeting picture of a broken pane may suffice. The physician and naturalist Erasmus Darwin (1731-1802; grandfather of Charles) had the same idea when he wrote:

> If any one should say "one may sit upon a horse safer than on a camel," my abstract idea of the two animals includes only an outline of the level back of the one, and the gibbosity on the back of the other. What noise is that in the street?— some horses trotting over the pavement. Here my idea of the horses includes principally the shape and motion of their legs.[16]

Thus what we call the idea of a thing may be: (1) the entire potentiality of relevant associations; (2) the particular excerpt that plays a part in the peirasis; (3) the abbreviated representative that deputizes for the latter; or (4) some conventional symbol, a word or token. Of course, there are numerous intermediate possibilities, not to mention the changing phases and alternating aspects.

It is, then, clear from the very rapidity of thought processes that some greatly abridged substitute for the complete idea must replace it for most purposes. Such a substitute can function effectively as a representative of the real thing if the purpose of the reflection is limited. A hole has been discovered under a fence, and the question is asked: Can a dog have made it? The single memory of a dog making such a hole will answer the question and no further revival of the dog-idea is called for. Again, we have watched a football game and on the following day have to answer such a question as: What was the ground like? A brief recollection of the muddied players sliding about near the goal line will provide the answer. In fact the account of the ninety-minute game that could be constructed from the whole of our memories would be but the lightest sketch of the real sequence of events. We think we can recall the match because we can recall as much as we require.

But the point for the moment is not so much that our memories can in any case provide but a scanty representation of the reality; rather the point is that if our memory were complete it would be almost useless. The value of internal peirasis lies in the fact not only that we can review the past and foresee the future to some extent, but also that we can do so in a mere fraction of the time the real events have occupied or will occupy. This is possible because we do not recall more than what is relevant at any particular moment.

5 *Abstract and General Ideas*

It was early recognized that the sensations we receive from the objects of our environment sometimes recur in a modified form when those objects are not present; to account for such memories a notion of "mental images" was elaborated. Aristotle speaks of imagination as the faculty that supplies them.[17] This idea of a mental image was no doubt based on the experience of pictures and paintings. The imagined picture of a man was like a painting and served a similar purpose. It recalled the real man and could be studied at leisure.

The notion accounted fairly well for our ideas of particular objects but not for our ideas of types or classes. When I call up in my mind the image of a dog, it is the image of one particular dog. But when I reason about dogs, I am concerned with all the dogs that ever existed, and of this uncounted multitude I can form no image at all. Nevertheless I seem able to reason effectively about them and to form some sort of idea of the generalized dog as easily and rapidly as I form the image of an individual one. But this is not easy to explain. The image represents the particular dog because it resembles it. But what kind of an idea can it be that represents the whole class of dogs? It certainly cannot be one that resembles it.

This difficulty was the source of much medieval speculation and disputation. Since most reasoning is concerned with these "universals," as they were called, they were considered by many to be more important than the particulars. This was also Plato's view. Since it was agreed that ideas must represent something, it was impossible to believe that the most important of them all could represent nothing.

It may seem strange that so much was made of this difficulty about general ideas and so little about particular ones when in fact the difficulty is much the same. When an individual object is presented to our senses, we receive only one aspect at a time, and when the number of aspects is very large it may be as hard for us to experience them all as to get to know all the dogs in the world. Even if the number of aspects is not impossibly large, how can we represent them in our minds simultaneously? It is surely no easier than condensing a thousand dogs into a single image. Indeed it is less easy, for any two dogs have much in common, while two aspects of a dog may have very little. Yet for some reason this difficulty did not strike the philosophers for a long time.

Moreover, when I think about X and reason about him I am not dependent exclusively on my memories of *him*. Though I know him well, I have never seen him shaving or in his bath. Yet I have little difficulty in picturing him in either situation. For this purpose I draw on my experience of myself and other people. I cannot really separate my knowledge of X from my knowledge of other men, and often I could not say, in respect to some particular fact about him, whether I learned it from observation of him or inferred it from observation of others. Persons we do not know particularly well are represented in our minds by memories derived to an even less extent from themselves. There is Z whom I often see in the street though I have never spoken to him. I can make him the subject of my thoughts and take account of his probable actions in various circumstances. If I can do this with some confidence it is on the strength of my experience of other people. As soon as I have recognized him as a man I transfer to him the great mass of experience I have built up from the observation of men who resemble him.

Thus it is with all the familiar objects of our environment. Our ideas of them are only in part derived directly from experience of the objects themselves: to a greater or less extent they are derived from other objects and then transferred to these, and it would seldom be possible to say in any particular case how much of our idea of a thing came from one source and how much from another. Although it may be theoretically quite possible to distinguish historically between my experiences of X and my experiences of Y and Z, it certainly does not follow that the memories of these experiences remain distinct in the brain. On the contrary, it is certain that similar experiences are in general confounded and amalgamated in one single memory, if memory is the appropriate term. This does not imply that any composite image is formed, for knowledge of a thing is not dependent on the power of forming an image of it. One may know how to deal with an object in its presence and yet be unable to visualize it at all clearly. To have an adequate idea of a thing means, as a rule, to know how to deal with it. At the same time, when an image *is* formed, it may be derived from any of the stock of similar experiences and may even in some cases be composite.

Thus, if by the *idea* of a thing we mean all the revivable memories of it, then there can be no clear distinction between a particular idea and a general one. Both represent a collection of potential images or thoughts, and it is impossible to say that some collections are made up exclusively of memories of one particular thing. If, on the other hand, by idea we understand the momentary represenation in the mind during internal peirasis, then still more clearly there can be no distinction between the particular and the general, since such difference as exists must depend upon the associated memories that remain potential.

It is common to draw a distinction between general and abstract ideas. The idea of an insect or bird is general, since there are certain definable characters common to all birds, as to all insects, although it is impossible to form any mental picture of them. We cannot picture a bird that does not have some of the characters of a particular species; and when we come to think of the common characters, we are compelled to picture them in one or another of the concrete forms they assume in a particular species. If we are ornithologists with an extensive knowledge of birds of all kinds, we shall be able to substitute very quickly one form for another in our imagination, as the purposes of our reflective process require. It is this power of calling up at need any of a large number of different concrete examples that makes profitable thinking with general ideas possible. There are, on the other hand, characters that do appear to be separately thinkable. The words *red, hard, cold* denote characteristics that are associated with all kinds of quite different things; and although we do not suppose that they denote anything that could exist apart from *some* object, yet we seem to be able to think of them apart. I can imagine the color red, the sensation of hardness or cold, without having to imagine any kind of object at all. It is such characteristics as these that are usually called abstract. But in fact they are merely more easy to picture and therefore attention has been drawn to them more quickly.

Why can we think of these characteristics apart, in spite of the unlimited variety of the objects with which they are in reality associated, whereas we find it extremely difficult to think of the common character of all insects apart, although the number of species known to most of us is much smaller? The answer involves the nature of our sensory apparatus. The eye has a faculty for distinguishing colors, as the skin has for distinguishing temperatures. These are *elementary* sensations, and we know whether we are experiencing them or not without regard to any other accompanying sensations. We can imagine ourselves enveloped in a red cloud that obliterates all forms and excites only our color sense. We can imagine ourselves exposed to different temperatures while in complete darkness and experiencing no other sensations. Hardness and softness must probably always be associated with some part of our own body but not with any other sensation of the surrounding world. It is the simplicity of these sensations that makes it possible for us to experience them in isolation and therefore to imagine them in isolation. We can picture to ourselves only what we can actually feel, and our imagination is derived from our sensory experience. It is within our power to rearrange in our imagination the elements of our experience, but we cannot go beyond it to imagine elements that have never been "given" to us in experience.

There is, then, no fundamental distinction between general and abstract ideas; both are commonly involved in what is called abstract thinking. We have to collect out of numerous, perhaps remote, contexts in memory the separate items of experience that are related to one problem and will be required for our internal experimentation. Such items may have to be drawn from memories of events and situations far apart in place and time. It is only because the original, continuous train of experience may be carved up in the mind and applied a little at a time, as required, that we can piece together disconnected fragments of experience and out of them construct the things and processes with which, in internal peirasis, we have to operate. The flexibility of the materials of thought is due to the power of abstraction, the power that enables us, for the purposes of internal explorations, not only to dismember the complex situations of our experience so as to be able to rearrange their components but also to separate the qualities and attributes of material objects.

Ideas of the attributes of a thing arise from thinking about it only under the particular aspect that is relevant to the immediate problem. When we are seeking an implement with which to do a particular job, we review a number of likely objects in our imagination, but in thinking of each one in turn we have only to picture that particular part or aspect that is relevant to the job. A stone is used at one time because it is heavy, at another because it is hard, at yet another because it has a sharp edge or a point. For each of these purposes it may be replaced by something else. A receptacle filled with earth may be equally heavy, a piece of bone or horn may seem as hard, and a split cane may be as sharp. The use of alternatives, the comparison of methods and tools and materials in actual applications, brings the attention more and more to the particular quality that happens to be in request. The quality is not to be found, of course, except in some object; but when a series of objects has been found, distinct in origin, in material, and in all other characters, yet alike in the possession of the one quality—capable, in fact, of being graded according to the degree in which they possess it—then the quality begins to have an independent representation in the mind.

This, however we may imagine such representation to be accomplished, constitutes an abstraction. Sharpness is the quality in a tool that makes it useful for cutting, and when we think of sharpness we do not have to think of a knife, chisel, axe, or a razor but only of the cutting process or its effects. In our mental calculations we do not have to review the whole range of edged tools in order to reckon with the possibility of separating into parts a solid piece of matter. With the aid of such abstractions it becomes possible to work out an operation in internal peirasis in terms of such entities as "something sharp" or "something heavy," "something tough and flexible." Without stopping to imagine any particular object or material, confident in the conviction that such things can easily be found, and carrying in one's mind an image of the effect rather than of the thing, one may bring one's mental experiment to a successful issue. There is not even any need for a word. The mind is quite capable of disembodying the quality and using it in its incorporeal form. When one of Köhler's chimpanzees goes in quest of a stick or box, he knows the kind of thing he wants. But from the variety of objects he will accept and try out, it is evident that he may carry in his mind ideas of qualities rather than of particular objects. Thus he uses (as substitutes for a stick when none is available) branches torn from trees, metal bars broken from a shoe-scraper, screwed-up bundles of straw, and so forth. He knows, then, that what he wants has to be of a certain length, width, weight, and rigidity; and each object that presents itself is judged to be appropriate or not in the light of this knowledge.

An attribute is not, of course, the same as an aspect. The aspect of a thing is that which may be presented through any or all of the senses at any one time. The attribute is that which has relevance in a particular situation. The color of an object, its shape, weight, and movements are attributes, but each may present several different aspects. The weight of a man, for example, produces quite a different sensory impression when we try to lift him and when he sits on our chest. Hence the attribute may be recognized by many different signs like the object or the event to which it belongs. A single aspect cannot fully represent the attribute any more than it can fully represent any real thing; nevertheless the attribute is usually very much simpler than the object, and the task of representing it mentally is correspondingly easier. This is especially the case where the attribute is subjective; for we may make a provisional distinction between the real qualities of an object and our own reaction or attitude towards them—between such qualities as weight, size, and shape, which seem to admit of precise definition, and those like beauty and goodness and truth, which do not. We can easily visualize a pretty face but not the prettiness without the face. Yet the emotional effect of a pretty face is to a large extent independent of the particular face and can be imagined without visualizing any face at all. In the same way our feelings about a thing, desire for it, sense of the need it would satisfy, the pleasure it would give, the pain it would allay, are subjective qualities that may represent it in our thoughts under a single aspect. Since these subjective qualities may be common to a great number of different real objects, that is to say, since a great number of different real objects produce in us the same feelings, subjective qualities of this kind may constitute a highly condensed representation of a considerable class of objects. It may commonly be observed that although general propositions are expressed in terms implying an objective classification, the real basis of classification is often emotional.

The subjective quality need not always involve what is generally understood by emotion. What, in the first place, makes two things alike for an animal is the fact that they are *equivalent* in relation to his needs and behavior. Similarity of behavior does not necessarily imply similarity of external situation. Two things may be objectively quite different and yet, for a particular animal or for an animal in particular circumstances, be equivalent; and he may profitably treat them as if they were the same. If he reacts to a situation or to an object because of some relation the object bears to him, then any other situation, however different in other respects, which bears the same relation, may come to elicit the same reactions. Where animals learn to deal with their environment by external peirasis, each situation comes independently to evoke its appropriate response; and since the repertoire of every animal is limited, it is inevitable that the same reaction should sometimes get linked to different stimuli. Since the appropriateness of a reaction does not in most cases depend on the nature of the sensory stimuli but on the physical or physiological facts of which they are merely the signs, and since the same vital facts may be signalled by quite different stimuli, it would be surprising if similarity of reaction were always correlated with similarity of stimulus.

In giving names to things we often act in the same way. To a great variety of objects, both simple and complex, we give the name *tool*, and we could no doubt give a good reason for classing so many different objects together; but it would not be because of any physical feature, shape, material, or movement they have in common but merely because of our manner of making use of them. When we form the general idea of a tool, machine, or gadget, it is not the shape we think of but the function, the use, the need, or the application; and we can often think of these in terms of our own body, our own movements, aims, or desires. It is much easier to think in such terms. When we hold a thing in our hands we mold our skin and muscles about it in such a way that we have an instantaneous feeling of its shape, which vision alone could furnish only after a succession of views from different points. When we sit on a horse or a bicycle we have an instantaneous sensation of shape, which vision can give only by association. These instantaneous though highly complex sensations are as easily imagined as any visual or auditory pattern.

Thus we form an idea of what is common to many different things by representing to ourselves our posture, our movements, or our emotional relation to them. In this way we find a substitute that is more readily conceived yet which represents the real thing adequately within the limits required.

The process of becoming acquainted with the world is a process of separating from the first chaos that surrounds us those things, acts, events, changes, qualitites, and movements that appear to concern us. It is reasonable to suppose that this process began at an early stage of evolution, when animals first reacted to something more complex than a specific sensory stimulus, when first they recognized the existence of things and situations that might be represented under different aspects. Situations were further analyzed into things and things into components. As the recognizable things grew more numerous, their resemblances and differences became more significant, and qualities were in turn separated from the things. Although the process has been carried much further by man, it is still the same process. The determining condition for each step in this progressive analysis is some specific form of behavior, and the chemist, like the ape, can only distinguish new things and new characteristics that bear some relation to his manipulations. But the discovery that many things may serve the same purpose or be made of the same substance or have the same shape or execute the same movements has led to the recognition of certain categories that are useful as a guide both in description and in construction. Most animals make discoveries only by accident, but man has learned to apply himself to the work of invention; the business of designing and making things has taught him to analyze the world into substance and quality, form and composition, structure and motion.

If internal peirasis is to terminate in effective action, sooner or later the disembodied abstraction must clothe itself in some concrete reality. In thinking out a method of accomplishing some design we may reflect that all we need is something sharp. With that reflection we reckon that part of our plan easy to accomplish, and we go on to work out the remainder of it. Perhaps nothing actually passed through our mind but the word *sharp*, which sufficed at that stage and permitted the process to be contemplated as a whole. But when it comes to execution the word must be translated into something material, and the sharpness must be represented by some effective tool. As long as the abstraction, or the word which stands for it, can when necessary be translated into concrete terms, the word may be said to have a meaning—its meaning being just this translation. Where such translation is impossible or where the number of possible translations is indefinite, the meaning is nonexistent or so vague as to be no better than nonexistent. This will not matter if, as is so often the case in human behavior, the whole intellectual operation is to end in nothing but words. In that case the abstractions may remain as unsubstantial and the peirasis be as undisciplined as one chooses.

6 *Speculative Thinking, Symbolism in Thinking, and Wishful Thinking*

Philosophers have been inclined to emphasize the contemplative rather than the active features of thought. But for most people who lead an active life thought must be largely concerned with their own possible actions. It is not possible to think of any familiar object or place or person except in some relation to ourselves. When I try to recall St. Paul's Cathedral I find myself viewing it from some particular position, looking up from St. Paul's Churchyard or from the bottom of Ludgate Hill. I cannot think of the cathedral except by putting myself somewhere in sight of it. One may overlook this element in memory as one may ignore it during the actual perception; in this way human knowledge becomes, with increasing sophistication, less directly concerned with one's possible actions. The natural, or perhaps we should say the primitive, function of reflection is to make unnecessary the expenditure of time and energy on random trials. Various possible actions are reviewed and their effects imagined, and we spare ourselves in this way the physical exertions and also sometimes the danger of testing the effects by actual experiment. But how was there developed from this that more abstract kind of thinking that appears to be concerned with no conceivable action but merely with questions of truth and reality, not with what we can do in a situation but with merely ascertaining what the situation is?

We have seen that man and other mammals must build up a representation of their immediate environment in their minds. At any moment they can only *see* what lies before their eyes, but they require to *know* a good deal of what is not in sight. It is against the background of this mental representation that they react in each particular contingency. The effective environment of man is much larger than that of most other animals, not merely in geographical extent but in complexity and multiplicity of significant elements, and his mental representation of the environment is correspondingly more complex. Since the environment is not constant and invariable the picture must be kept up to date. Situations not open to brief visual survey may require long periods for their exploration, and if the successive observations are to be summed finally, the earlier ones must be retained until the exploration is complete.

Furthermore, if the situation is not perfectly static, those parts that were investigated at the beginning may have changed before the later parts are reached, and if our final picture, based on a protracted process of exploration, is to represent the actual state of affairs, we must make allowance for such changes. Our ability to do so obviously depends on our knowledge of regular sequences. When we are acquainted with certain processes, we assume that they take place in our absence as well as in our presence. If therefore in our exploration we find such a sequence in progress, we allow for the normal process when we come to the final integration of our findings. To some extent other animals must necessarily perform the same feat; but in man the extent of the situations that interest him and the time required to explore them and ascertain their structure have greatly increased the importance of this adjustment. And man, having long ago become aware of this importance, has devoted a great deal of energy to the task of ascertaining as many natural sequences as possible. In this way, knowledge has come to be more contemplative and less active.

The invention of language in its various forms has had the effect of enlarging the range of every individual's senses. We can see with each other's eyes and share each other's memories. It is obvious enough that we could not have got very far without these aids to cooperation; but every advance of this kind consists in extending the range of inference and has therefore increased the possibilities of error and illusion. Our neighbor speaks words; we have to infer from them what his ideas are, and our inferences may be seriously wrong.

From a consideration of the way in which ideas are formed it is obvious how difficult must be their communication merely by the use of words. The most that can be done by means of a definition is to give instructions for the formation of an idea, to direct a person to the experiences from which it must be derived. If I say that an insect is an arthropod with six legs, a tubular tracheal system, a single pair of antennae, and so forth, I am not contributing very much to the direct formation of an idea of insects, but I am giving directions for their recognition, just as I might say that Mr. Smith is the man who lives at No. 65. If you want to form an adequate idea of the gentleman, you must call on him and study him. My instructions merely guide you to the study of the right person. If I try to do more than this—if I try, for instance, to convey my thoughts about the biology of insects or the character of Mr. Smith by purely verbal means—I may be contributing further erroneous or distorted ideas to the mind of my listener.

People, animals, common materials, furniture, and tools are in many cases known to us from constant intercourse throughout life, and we are confident that we can predict their behavior under all usual conditions. These, therefore, are the raw material of our thoughts, and we tend to make them serve as substitutes for everything more complex or less familiar. In larger contexts, or where more complex things are concerned, we cannot have the same amount of experience. Aspects are more numerous and repetitions less frequent. We know what a certain individual will do under most ordinary circumstances, but we cannot so easily predict the behavior of a crowd or a community. And so in our thoughts about the latter we substitute an individual. Historians, accounting for the vicissitudes of nations, parties, or sects, must in their meditations find some simpler substitute of dependable behavior; and it is often evident that while they speak of nations they are thinking about individuals. None of us, when we think of some political party, can picture the millions of individuals in their various environments, with their different experience, interests, knowledge, mentalities. We must think of some particular man or woman who symbolizes the party for us, and whose known behavior is ascribed to it as a whole. The best we can do is to let the representative individual vary. We cannot superpose Mr. X on Mr. Y, for the two characters are perhaps completely different. But if they are both identified in our mind with the party, we can take them alternately as our symbol and so avoid the more extreme forms of error. By reminding ourselves that many millions of people cannot all have the same purpose, the same ideal, the same illusions, and the same vices, we may check any rash predictions about the behavior of such a complex entity and partially suppress any strong emotional attitude toward it. Yet if the check were continually applied, our thinking would be so greatly hampered that we should barely be able to reach any general conclusions at all.

In making such substitutions we reduce the task of reflection within manageable limits but at the cost, naturally, of confidence in the results. In order that there may be any results at all, there must be some relation between the reality and the substitute or symbol. In this way an individual man can be substituted for a crowd because the actions of a crowd can be compared to those of an individual and are generally described in the terms used for describing those of an individual. In scientific inquiries the greatest care is taken to ensure that the important properties of the real thing are shared by the substitute. But in unscientific (and this includes a great deal of so-called philosophical) reflection, no special precautions are taken, because the process is not deliberate and often not conscious. And then, of course, the conclusions reached with the aid of symbols have no necessary bearing on the real problem under investigation.

The part played by symbols in dreams has been made familiar by Sigmund Freud, and was previously recognized, according to Freud, by the English psychologist, Havelock Ellis (1859–1939).[18] The figures and situations and events that occur in dreams can often be traced to more complex and less easily representable ideas that have been replaced. Freud was primarily concerned with the substitution that suppressed certain thoughts the "censor" would not pass. But he recognized that symbolism was a more general phenomenon. On this subject he quotes the German psychologist Herbert Silberer, who observed that if, at the moment of falling asleep, he was engaged with some more or less abstract thought, a transformation would take place by which the elements of the abstract thought would be converted into concrete images.[19] By rousing oneself just before dropping off to sleep one may detect the change. Freud gives some of Silberer's examples:

> I am thinking of how I must improve an awkward passage in an essay. Symbol: I see myself planing a piece of wood. . . . I am trying to realize the purpose of certain metaphysical studies on which I am just about to embark. This purpose consists, so it seems to me, in seeking the foundations of Being by working one's way up to ever higher forms of consciousness and strata of experience. Symbol: I am poking a long knife under a tart as if to partake of a portion.[20]

It is not, of course, only in a state of semiconsciousness that this transformation occurs, but in the dream state the symbols are more grotesque. It will be noticed, for example, that in the preceding quotation the words in which the original thought is expressed are almost as concrete as the "symbol." "Seeking the foundations" of a thing or "working one's way up to ever higher forms" through "strata of experience" are readily conceived as concrete processes even though the words *form* and *experience* have, of course, no representable meaning. Freud recognized that this symbolical thinking was not restricted to dreams, for he says:

> Dream-elaboration accomplishes nothing novel by this kind of substitution. For the attainment of its purposes, in this case evasion of the censor, it only follows paths already laid down in unconscious thought, giving preference to those transformations of the repressed material which may be allowed to become conscious as jokes or allusions and of which the fantasies of neurotics are full.[21]

The process is well illustrated by this very passage. The *Traumarbeit* seeking to evade the censor, following the beaten track in unconscious thought and preferring one disguise to another, is almost as crude and concrete a substitute for any scientific psychological conception as Silberer helping himself to a portion of tart.

But of course it is inevitable. In all our thinking we must substitute concrete and figured ideas for the complex entities with which we are really concerned, whenever these reach a certain degree of magnitude and complication. Simple objects, actions, and processes are the only ones that admit of approximately integral representation. In all other cases we must make do with a partial view or, if we need to consider the object as a whole, we must replace it by something that can find room in our imagination. We can only think effectively with the things with which we are familiar; every symbol therefore must be borrowed from experience. The substitution occurs spontaneously. Even when we clothe our thoughts in abstract terms it is often quite evident that they are behaving like familiar concrete things. We speak of France, of civilization, of art, or of science, but since we cannot really think of such vast complexes we silently substitute a map, a formula, a picture, or a crucible. As we have seen, in thinking of the affairs of a state, of the relations between different sections of the population, of the effects of administrative measures, we think of one or two familiar individuals and make them deputize in our reflections for classes we suppose them to represent. When we suppose ourselves to be contemplating the destiny of nations, we are in fact watching a puppet show made up from the scanty materials of our own narrowly circumscribed experience.

The vast extension of the range of human interests both in space and in time has greatly increased the possibilities of error and illusion. As the aims of men comprehend remote objects and involve calculations concerning conditions distant in time and space, and as the attainment of the goal is removed further and further in time from the initiation of an enterprise, the connection between an action and its effects becomes loose and uncertain. In many cases the ultimate effects of a man's actions are unknown. His purpose may or may not have been achieved. Yet that purpose may be of such a nature that he is satisfied by believing that it has. A feeling of security is as desirable as a feeling of warmth or health, and if the feeling can be induced by a belief, then behavior may be directed toward establishing the belief rather than the reality.

So it comes about that the most elaborate constructions in the human mind may provide, instead of a faithful representation of the actual situation, a reassuring representation of a desirable one. Such comforting illusions would be of no value to an animal whose concern for the future did not extend beyond the immediate range of its senses, for they would so soon be dispelled. But a man's happiness depends on remote conditions and on conditions whose existence can often be revealed only after a long interval or in particular circumstances; it is therefore determined by belief much more than by perception. We wish to be loved or admired. If we can convince ourselves that we *are* loved or admired we are content. Of course, all people do not have this power of convincing themselves against the evidence of other persons' opinions, but by selecting one's associates one may bias the evidence. In any case people's feelings, agreeable or otherwise, depend in the main on their beliefs and not on the facts. Knowledge may enable one to change an unfavorable situation, but belief may enable one to enjoy it. Where ignorance is bliss, 'tis folly to be wise!

Moreover, many unpleasant situations cannot be changed. The story of the ostrich who averts danger by burying his head in the sand is a biological absurdity; individuals who evinced such a tendency would be quickly eliminated. But it is different in the case of man. Although it is perilous for man, too, to ignore an imminent evil, it may be better for him to remain ignorant of a distant one. It is better to live in ignorance than in dread. And so the process of reconstructing in one's imagination the real situation may serve another purpose than the practical one of dealing with it appropriately. It may be more important for our peace of mind, or for our vanity, to believe that the situation is as we wish it than to know what in fact it is. The process of internal peirasis is as readily directed to this end as to the other. This is what Rignano called "intentional reasoning." It is more familiarly termed "wishful thinking." We manipulate our thoughts not with a view to finding a way of mending a situation but in order to convince ourselves that it needs no mending. Such reasoning may be employed to convince others rather than oneself, but then it is no longer merely internal peirasis. The advocate constructing his case, the politician defending his policy, the believer justifying his faith illustrate in a familiar form the perverted reasoning that proceeds silently in most men's minds when they start to reason about either their tenets or their interest.

Thus, speculative thinking passes from the service of practical needs to the safeguarding of inward harmony. Other animals can have little use for such thinking, for what is within their perceptual range requires prompt action, and what is beyond it brings them neither comfort nor misgiving. Thus we do not expect to find any traces of religion or philosophy among the lower mammals. Man, on the other hand, explores in his imagination the whole universe—past, present, and future—and where he cannot or need not test the validity of his constructions, he builds as he is prompted by his desires and his fears. He could not long continue to believe that he could live on air or that it never rains on Thursdays. But he might go through life believing that the sun is not much bigger than the moon. And where beliefs concern the remote past or the remote future there is, in the case of most men, little to prevent them believing almost anything.

7 *Reason and Emotion: Generalized and Specialized Instincts*

No conscious act can be called purely rational if this means that emotion plays no part in it. The rational element in behavior is that part of the mechanism which guides the animal to its goal; but the goal must exert some kind of attraction before this mechanism can be brought into play. If it were not for the affective attitude of man toward his environment (his fears and desires), there would be nothing to explain the adaptive character of his theories or why he should attend to one event rather than another, nothing for him to reason about, nothing to excite his curiosity, direct his thoughts, or prevent them from meandering aimlessly in an endless reverie. The reasoning process is one by which a man seeks ways and means of satisfying his desires or eluding danger. It is continually guided by his needs, so much so that it is sometimes frustrated by their importunity. To attribute a man's actions to reason is to imply that he has a motive, and this presupposes a desire or a fear.

The so-called conflict between "reason" and "passion," when it occurs, is really between one passion and another. In a novel situation, for instance, the passion of fear may prompt us to withdraw while the passion of curiosity leads us to explore further. Reason, in such a case, is merely the imagination, which draws on our memories to predict the consequences of either course of action. Reason is the same as imagination except that we use the latter term where no strong aim or desire determines the sequence of images or memories. When we are under the influence of a desire or fear (not so strong as to turn our behavior into panic), then there is a kind of selection of memories; this is called *reasoning.* When there is no such selective guidance of what we recall, we call the process *imagination* or *daydreaming.*

To explain the role of emotion in guiding human behavior, I must say a little about the behavior of the lower animals and how it differs from that of vertebrates, particularly from that of mammals.

The behavior of many lower animals is so nicely adjusted to the normal environment in which they occur that their inherited equipment suffices for all their needs. The individual does not have to learn anything, and is in fact incapable of doing so. If anything happens to it for which it possesses no natural inherited response, it comes to grief. Even insect behavior is subject to improvement only to a very limited degree. The solitary wasp, *Ammophila,* paralyzes a caterpillar with its sting, drags it to a hole it has previously dug, lays its eggs on it, and then blocks the hole. When the grubs hatch, the caterpillar, paralyzed but not killed, is their first meal. The parent wasp can have no conception of the purpose of this series of activities, which it repeats again and again, and it will never see the next generation for which its behavior has thus provided. It does not *learn* to perform the series but is prompted from the first by inherited instincts. It is, however, impossible to dismiss such behavior as the purely mechanical repetition of a fixed sequence. The site of the burrow must be chosen and remembered, and the caterpillar dragged to it from the spot where it is captured. The conditions are not absolutely identical on any two occasions, and if the insect were simply a blind mechanism, it would take no account of these variations in the environment. That it in fact does so means that there is a certain amount of variability in its behavior.

With a mammal, this variability has increased enormously; its instincts do not prompt it to perform a stereotyped series of almost invariable actions. We may say that whereas insects and other invertebrates as a rule appear to know of only one means of satisfying each of their needs, the mammal may know of several and is often able to discover new ones. The spider must wait until a suitable victim becomes enmeshed in its web before it can attack and eat it. It cannot, when the normal supply fails, set out and adopt new methods, such as lying in ambush by the wayside or diving below water in quest of a water boatman. But when a fox is hungry, its prelusive behavior varies within quite wide limits, and the sequence of acts it performs before it reaches a situation in which it can eat is far from stereotyped. The fox's behavior is guided by its hunger, but only in a generalized way.

The animal whose instincts are specialized has an extremely effective apparatus for dealing with certain normal situations; a highly complex sequence of behavior occurs, all the elements of which are fixed. In the generalized instinct the complexity of a particular action is due to the ad hoc combination of a large number of independently variable elements. In one case the whole is prefabricated; in the other it is made up from small parts as required. A generalized instinct may be less effective in a particular situation than a specific one; in other circumstances adaptability is often more useful than adaptation.

This classification of animals into those whose behavior is stereotyped and those whose instinctive tendencies are more generalized is, as already suggested, not absolute. Not only do insects and similar animals exhibit experimental behavior to some extent, but every mammal possesses very precise and constant reflexes, which are the very type of automatic behavior. I shall argue in a later chapter that what is called "play" is, in its simplest and most primitive form, merely undirected activity. It is, at least, less definitely or consistently directed toward any specific goal than other forms of behavior, but does not differ essentially from these. In the whole range of behavior it may be regarded as lying at the opposite extreme to the reflex. The latter is fixed and invariable down to the very sequence and combination of muscular contractions. The former is not even related to any consistent end at all. Between these extremes are to be found all forms of instinctive and intelligent behavior, the latter by their variability and spontaneity partaking in greater or less degree of the nature of play, and the former by their more stereotyped character approaching the reflex.

Psychologists draw a distinction between instinctive and intelligent behavior; by the latter they mean such behavior as is prompted by generalized instincts. The intelligent animal is one that learns in time to link the most suitable response to each particular situation. Its prelusive behavior when prompted by hunger or any other instinct is essentially experimental in character. Instead of an automatic response to a particular stimulus there is groping and experiment. The same actions may easily be performed under the prompting of entirely different instincts. Putting on my hat and coat and setting out to catch a train may be a prelude to satisfying my hunger in a restaurant or my literary ambition in a library. It is this vagueness about behavior associated with the human instincts that has led to the great divergence of opinion among psychologists in dealing with them. Some recognize comparatively few, others multiply them almost indefinitely. But in spite of this general vagueness there are certain states of tension in mammals generally which, although they do not prompt any uniform line of conduct, may be described as leading to behavior that *converges* on a particular final act or situation. However variable the prelusive phase, there is a characteristic conclusion that brings the experimental process to an end.

I shall refer to these states of tension as *drives* They are related to the fundamental needs of the animal, whose survival depends on avoiding dangerous situations and maintaining a state of physiological equilibrium. The actions the animal performs for these purposes vary according to its specific structure, but, speaking generally, we may say that it must eat, drink, breathe, and dispose of waste. Dangerous situations announce themselves to its external senses, and appropriate action is thus prompted by the external situation. Lack of food or drink or oxygen announce themselves by a change in the internal situation, and as a rule these internal needs give rise to a drive. If the lack can be made good by some change of behavior that is not specifically related to the external situation, there may be a reflex response. This is the case sometimes when there is a lack of oxygen. But lack of food or drink will usually call for a train of activity whose details and sequence depend on the actual environment. When the need can be immediately satisfied by an appropriate action—as is generally the case in elimination—the drive hardly arises, or has no distinct role. But where the need is one that can only be satisfied in an appropriate situation, then the function of the drive is to prompt the animal to action. The particular character of the drive will determine to some extent the nature of the activity, but only within rather wide limits. The drive initiates and maintains the peirasis and gives it a general directive.

The drive arises as a result of some internal disequilibrium, which may either be the climax of some slowly maturing condition or the sudden consequence of an environmental disturbance. It arises when there is no response available to meet the case in the presence of the existing external situation. Steps must be taken to *alter* the situation or the animal's relation to it, before any action can be performed that directly removes the source of disturbance or reestablishes equilibrium. The drive persists until either the external disturbing condition has been removed or the internal equilibrium has been restored. The former is often achieved by the attainment of a particular external situation. If an animal is attacked or threatened, the drive will persist until the attack has been repulsed or the attacker destroyed. On the other hand the internal state of equilibrium may be restored by some specific act, and in this case the drive persists until the conditions are reached in which that act may be performed.

In the latter case the action that releases the state of tension—that is, that resolves the drive—is often called a *consummatory act.* In the former case there is no specific consummatory act but rather a *releasing situation.* In some cases the unfavorable conditions may be not local but widespread, as when an animal is exposed to cold or overtaken by floods. Resolution of the drive will then depend upon the attainment of a more or less specific situation, a warm shelter or dry land. Where the releasing situation is highly specific, as when an animal is seeking its own nest, the final acts of the sequence that leads to it may also be specific so that there is a releasing situation and a consummatory act.

The more specific the drive, the more restricted in general will be the range of peirasis. In human psychology this difference is sometimes indicated by the terms *feeling* and *emotion*. The former is more definite and directs us at once to a certain limited range of behavior. When we feel cold or have a pain in the foot, we take measures of a more or less definite character related to the nature of the disturbance. But when we feel sad or jealous or angry, we experience far more miscellaneous promptings, and our experiments may range over a wide field of activity.

The drive, as already noted, is related to some fundamental need of the animal. But this relation may be indirect. Man's fundamental needs are not so very different from those of other animals. The difference in behavior is due to the more elaborate ways in which man exploits his environment for their satisfaction, and in the less direct relation between his most effective drives and those needs. The process of bringing into existence the releasing situation becomes more protracted as the animal learns indirect ways of attaining its object. Where this can be accomplished only in stages there tends to develop a series of secondary drives that must be resolved in turn by successive situations that form, as it were, stepping stones on the way to final resolution and the satisfaction of the fundamental need. It is as if the primary state of tension were able to shed a kind of luster on any prelusive goal that had, by association, become linked to it and to its resolution.

Let us take a common case. A man studies for a degree he desires, not for anything that can be done with the paper he receives from the university but perhaps because it will enable him to apply for a post. After the examination he goes to hear the result, and his emotion is so intense that he trembles. When the good news is anounced he can scarcely contain himself. Yet this release of tension when he hears his name pronounced or sees it in print bears no describable relation to any instinctive requirement. The desire fulfilled can be described only as a prelusive aim. The man wants the degree for the sake of some prestige or power that it will give him, and this in turn is coveted for what it will enable him to do or win. We shall see (Chapter 9, p. 76) how the satisfaction felt at solving a stage of a problem can become, even for an ape, a source of pleasure in itself, without thought of the stage as a means to an end.

Because I am concerned in this book with invention and discovery, and the processes involved in reasoning and hypothesis, any analytical study of instincts is unnecessary. For knowledge is not in itself a biological end. It does not directly feed or protect us or prolong our lives. If we know how to make use of it it may help us to do all of these things, but it is a means and not an end. It may be pursued and accumulated by men who reap none of these benefits, and the benefits may be reaped by those who have none of the knowledge. In human society, therefore, there is no close connection between the acquisition of knowledge and the instincts that must be satisfied if life is to continue. The biologist must assume of course that there is always some connection, however indirect; but since the application of knowledge is not related to any one instinct more than to another, we need not inquire into the various instinctive tendencies in any detail in order to be able to investigate the general process of seeking and acquiring it.

This separation of the emotional and intellectual powers has been quite generally adopted by psychologists in the past, although they may not always have appreciated the considerations that justify such a course. There has frequently been an inclination to regard reason as something that functioned on a higher plane than the feelings and passions. Reason was supposed to be that which distinguished man from all other animals. Descartes made it the characteristic activity of the soul and assigned the emotions to the machine. But nowadays the tendency is rather to exaggerate the dependence of all rational processes on concealed desires or fears and to look for the hidden motive behind every outwardly logical inference. Unnatural appetites and insane terrors are often alleged to account for the most normal and seemingly reasonable acts. The idea of reason as something that permits an animal to adapt its behavior to its needs and situation is often treated as a ludicrous misconception. It is not surprising that certain philosophers should have taken fright and met the challenge by protesting that the fundamentals of logic have nothing whatever to do with psychological principles. For how could they claim to be unbiased seekers after truth if it were generally believed that their systems were merely the symbolic expression of their libido?

8 *Unconscious Thinking*

Everybody knows, or supposes that he knows, the difference between conscious, voluntary behavior and unconscious reflexes. The same outward stimulation of the senses organs may on one occasion give rise to a reaction of which we know nothing until it is accomplished, and on another produce a sensation but no reaction. This difference depends on what happens in the central nervous system. Conscious behavior always involves the cerebral cortex and associated structures in the brain. Without any reference to anatomical details, we may speak of this part of the brain as the *resonator*. The rest of the central nervous system, which includes the spinal cord, will for distinction be called the *operator*. Whenever the will is in action, or when there is conscious sensation, the resonator is involved.

Many reflexes, adjustments of posture, and the coordination of elements in a voluntary act, are organized exclusively in the operator. No complex *action* can be performed without the cooperation of the operator, but sensations, perceptions, reflection, and dreams may hardly involve the operator at all unless or until they issue in some kind of behavior. During normal activity the animal's sense organs, its eyes, ears, skin, and so forth, are continually being stimulated by the environment. This pattern of stimulation produces in the operator a corresponding pattern of excitation. Where there is only reflex activity and no consciousness, this stimulus directly evokes the appropriate act. Or it would perhaps be better to say that where this stimulus evokes an appropriate act directly, the act is said to be a reflex, and there is no consciousness. But under certain conditions, instead of evoking an action the stimulus exerts an influence on the resonator, where it produces what we are aware of as a sensation. Unless this occurs the stimulation of a sense organ produces no sensation.

Most psychologists have recognized that it is the automatic forms of behavior which are generally unconscious. The body is a complex machine, which differs however from most man-made ones, not only in its greater complexity but in being subject to adaptive modification that follows spontaneously from its experience in working. In other words animals learn to adapt their behavior to the conditions in which they work, whereas other machines do not, or only to a very slight extent. Now all animal behavior is not equally adaptable, and we can in general distinguish two kinds of behavior in all the more complex animals, the automatic and the experimental. It is through the latter that they learn.

Although the power to learn is of great value to an animal, it is just as important that it should not have to depend exclusively on experimental behavior. For it must be able in all common emergencies to act quickly and accurately without fumbling, and that part of its behavior related to the constant or regularly recurring conditions, either in the environment or inside the body, must be in constant harmony with them and adapted from moment to moment to their demands. The fact that the conditions are recurrent or constant makes a stereotyped form of behavior possible. Experiment is only called for where unusual conditions present themselves, and it is only possible when the situation is not too urgent, for experiment takes time.

It is easy to recognize in the behavior of almost any animal that there are some forms of behavior that are more stereotyped than others. I have already described the experimental type under the name of *peirasis.* We have seen in the previous chapter that peirasis normally comes to an end when the drive that initiated it is satisfied, and satisfaction of a drive tends to establish a habit. In this way experimental behavior gives way under suitable conditions to stereotyped behavior. But many forms of behavior, even in the higher animals, have this character of uniformity from the first, without any preliminary process of experiment or learning. The peristaltic movements of stomach and intestines, the chemical activities of liver and kidneys, and the pumping action of the heart, are stereotyped and automatic, and include no experimental element. This constancy of action is made possible by the constancy of the conditions; for where these do not change it is sufficient that the machinery should be adapted once and for all and left to itself. To some extent, of course, these visceral activities are affected by the experimental behavior of the animal. The heartbeat, for example, varies with the general activity of the body, which may be of the experimental kind. But the visceral movements are automatically linked to the other movements and do not share in the peirasis.

There is a similar relation between the general behavior of the animal and the muscular coordinating system. In the course of its manifold activities it may have to seek refuge up a tree, dive under water, defend itself against attack, leap, run, burrow, and so on; doing any of these things involves a complex sequence of limb movements that must be in perfect harmony. The contraction of one set of muscles must be balanced by the relaxing of their antagonists; each local movement must be supported by others that maintain the posture of the body, and the whole must be coordinated in accordance with the requirements of equilibrium. Here again, since the relations of anatomy, posture, and the conditions of equilibrium are constant for any particular animal, whatever its immediate goal and the nature of its behavior may be, all such coordinating mechanisms may be fixed and stereotyped. This is not to say that it is not extremely complex and must not take account of a very large number of variable factors, but there is no call for improvisation.

It is true that children and many kinds of young animals are born with imperfect powers of coordination, and we must suppose that there is peirasis in the early part of life; but, since the result will be almost exactly the same for every individual, it may be that the normal process of growth brings about the necessary development. Some degree of refinement always remains possible, and by training we gain more perfect coordination of our bodily movements. This however cannot conceal the fact that the greater part of this apparatus for the coordination of movement is automatic in its action.

Almost any kind of behavior, every combination or sequence of actions, may become habitual, and the habitual action is automatic like the reflex action. As a result of peirasis and the resolution of a drive, a definite form of behavior becomes linked like a reflex to certain external and internal conditions, so that when those conditions arise the reaction occurs automatically.

Now it is a matter of general observation that all these forms of behavior, insofar as they are automatic, may also be unconscious. Much of our visceral behavior is always unconscious, at least when it is normal. Our coordinating movements are for the most part quite unknown to us until we make a special effort to observe them, and our habitual actions are frequently performed without our knowing it. It may be objected that our instinctive actions that are largely automatic are nevertheless conscious. But it must be remembered that in mammals the instincts are generalized and depend on the presence of a drive that determines a certain kind of behavior but not, except in the consummatory act, a stereotyped sequence. There is in nearly all cases a period of peirasis before the resolving situation is reached.

There is another point to be borne in mind. Our instinctive and reflex actions may be in themselves unconscious and yet observed by us objectively. Thus we can become aware of the beating of our heart by watching the pulse, and every reflex which is not under our control may come under our observation. Thus we may be said to become conscious of what are essentially unconscious acts. That they are essentially unconscious appears from the fact that they may be on other occasions perfectly performed without our knowing anything about them.

C. Lloyd Morgan (1852-1936), an English zoologist, held that the best criterion for conscious behavior was evidence that the animal profits by experience.[22] This might merely mean that consciousness is associated with peirasis, for it is only by means of peirasis that an animal can learn. Other psychologists have insisted on the role of consciousness in learning. We may suppose that following a successful act of external peirasis the nervous mechanisms involved in the act are reinforced and facilitated each time it is repeated. The easier an action becomes and the quicker the resolution of a state of internal tension, the less emotion will be felt, and the less will the conscious mind be concerned in the matter. The French psychologist F. Paulhan (1856-1931) suggested that consciousness and emotion arise when the animal's natural tendencies are arrested or obstructed.[23] The English philosopher Herbert Spencer (1820–1903). attempted to express a similar idea in physiological terms.[24] Where the sensory input to the nervous system leads rapidly and easily to a motor output, the sequence does not enter consciousness—that is, it does not involve the "higher" centers. Spencer is concerned to show under what conditions the nervous impulses are able, or compelled, to seek the "higher" centers.

If we now turn to internal peirasis, we may expect that similar conditions will determine when it is conscious and when not. Where there is no internal but only external peirasis the feeling is associated with the action and its goal. Where there is internal peirasis the feeling is associated with the ideas that replace the actions and the goal. But just as there are automatic actions unaccompanied by feeling or emotion, so there may be sequences of ideas without feeling or emotion if they are automatic. Both kinds of activity will be in themselves unconscious, but though the outward actions of the body may be objectively observed, the unconscious ideas will not be able to advertise themselves in the same way and are much more likely to be overlooked by psychologists. We can in some measure observe our own unconscious *actions,* catch ourselves doing things we had not intended, and in this way experience the difference between a conscious and an unconscious act. But when our *mental* processes become stereotyped and fade into unconsciousness, their continued existence can no longer be confirmed by any kind of direct observation but only by inference from our conscious conclusions. It is difficult, therefore, in recalling the course of our own reflections, to separate the conscious from the unconscious phases. We think we recall the latter when in fact we have only inferred them.

When all is said, it remains impossible to account for the effectiveness of thought in terms of those elements of idea and feeling we are able to trace in our consciousness. The mental experiment is often accomplished in a much shorter time than would be required for the real experiment, and many essential phases seem, upon introspection, never to have been represented at all. Yet every day every normal person performs this inexplicable feat of internal peirasis and demonstrates his success by his behavior.

I will conclude with a brief summary. The achievements of internal peirasis that seem so remarkable when we interrogate our memory become a little more intelligible when we take account of unconscious mental processes as well as unconscious actions. If unconsciousness is normal where an activity is highly organized and stereotyped, it is to be expected that habitual mental processes will also tend to become unconscious. Although we cannot, on the present theory, suppose that internal peirasis can ever be quite unconscious, yet there is a coordinating system in thinking which corresponds to that which controls outward activity. During external peirasis our movements are controlled and coordinated by nervous mechanisms involving the basal ganglia and cerebellum, which ensure that whatever we may try to do, we shall not fall into any kind of muscular incoherence that would defeat our aim. Of this control we know nothing because it is entirely automatic. Similarly, we may suppose that in internal peirasis a corresponding control is exercised, to prevent incoherence in our thoughts. But whereas the coordination of muscular activity is looked after by a mechanism whose structure is relatively fixed and permanent at an early age, the coordination of thought depends upon mechanisms (including parts of the cerebral cortex, hippocampus, and thalamus) that change and develop throughout life and are continuously being modified by experience and by the very thoughts and ideas to which they give rise.[25]

Part II

The Mind at Work and Play

9 *Invention*

The conditions in which human inventions and discoveries are made are very much the same, from the psychological point of view, as those described for chimpanzees by Köhler. The complexity is increased, but not their general nature. One factor, however, has gained enormously in importance—namely cooperation aided by language. Apes do not to any appreciable extent impart their discoveries to one another, nor do they learn from one another. In man this is indeed a new and fateful development. For whereas among apes it is the clever ones that solve the problems and get the rewards, among men, though it is still the clever ones who solve the problems, it is not only they who eat the bananas.

One significant development in human invention was a vast accumulation of erroneous beliefs and ineffectual practices. In the behavior of Köhler's apes there are examples of error and the misapplication of acquired skill; but such mistakes grow out of the individual's own experience and his own misjudgment. Among men the potent new factors of imitation and communication, while they make the inventions of the few available to the many, give rise also to the human specialities of myth and magic. For the ape, belief can only concern the structure of the present situation and can reach but a short way into the past, the future, or the remote. In consequence error, if not fatal, will generally be corrected. But where belief extends beyond the range of experimental testing there is little guarantee against illusion. Magic and hocus-pocus are however not the only byproducts of human invention, for man, like most mammals, is given to play, which consists essentially in repeating with endless variations all the more intricate operations an animal has learned to perform. To these topics I shall return. For the present we are concerned with the early growth of human invention, the practical adaptation of means to ends, for this was the foundation on which the whole intellectual development of humankind was raised.

Science has developed out of the observation of correlations between external things or events.[26] As the situations to which man's behavior was adapted became more extended and more complex, both in space and in time, the elements that attracted his attention became ever more removed from direct relation to his bodily actions and he became increasingly able to take an interest in external events and their relations to one another, without connecting them with himself. His social conditions favored this tendency, for in watching the behavior of his fellows he was in fact observing such external relations, even though one element in the relationship was a human being like himself. That this was one way in which he could be introduced to an objective view of things is suggested by the interest that chimpanzees, according to Köhler, may occasionally show in one another's performances.

Natural articles were always employed before it was possible to imagine manufactured substitutes. Before people could discover a way of making cloth they had to learn the uses of leaves, of bark, or of animal skins. Before they could conceive of pottery they had to learn the use of dried gourds and hollow plant stems. The invention of twine was preceded by the use of climbing plants or animal sinews. Before boats there were tree trunks, before houses, caves. This seems to be the general law of invention. Men first used implements and materials in the form in which nature provided them, and with such equipment they served their apprenticeship in all the arts and crafts. With increasing skill and expanding needs they grew more exacting and found out how to improve on the gifts of nature.

Much can be done—and in the beginning everything must be done—by external peirasis, by experimenting with the environment and with one's own body, whether in play or under the stress of necessity. The inventions of the ape are closely related to the immediate situation. But, as Köhler shows, there is sometimes an interval during which the animal seems to have ceased to concern itself with the problem it cannot solve, and yet it evidently carries in its mind some trace of the unresolved problem. For if during such an interval the ape's eyes happen to light on a possible tool it will at once abandon its apparent lethargy and, seizing the implement, return with new zest to the task. The idea of the unsolved problem must have survived in its mind when all external evidence of interest had ceased.

In man this interval may be longer. He can carry his problems about with him for indefinite periods, so that the terms of one may recur to him while he is engaged on the solution of another. When he is sawing or scraping with wooden tools he strikes fire, but this startling experience will lead to a discovery only if it finds waiting in his mind the necessary fructifying ideas—the uses of fire, the difficulty of procuring it at will, the labor and expense of maintaining it. In other words, some notion of the need must precede the discovery. The fact that clay can be molded and baked by the sun into a hard durable cake can be of no interest to the person who has no conception of the use of tiles or bricks or receptacles such as can be made out of this material. The ideas fertilized by the sight of sparks in the wood shavings, or of the clay baked in the sun, may be the result of some recent special experience or the permanent residue of chronic worries, or some unique experience recalled by luck at the right moment.

In such cases the indispensability of internal peirasis is evident. The experiences that in collaboration give significance to the discovery cannot occur together except in the memory. When we try to reconstruct the conditions that led to such early inventions as pottery and weaving, we have to imagine a succession of suggestive chances. We cannot suppose that the whole process, even at its simplest, could be provided at one time by a comprehensive accident. We cannot suppose that someone, amusing himself with a lump of clay, happened to produce a cup-shaped object, happened to put it in the fire, happened to take it out again when it had been baked, and then happened to find it useful as a receptacle. But combinations of material circumstance that cannot be expected to occur spontaneously may nevertheless be imagined. Separate experiences and operations, too slow and arduous to be by luck combined in the concrete, may be combined in the imagination in all kinds of possible and impossible ways. The mind is an imaginary workshop, and in times of quiet and leisure it is the scene of many novel experiments.

The whole of the circumstances relevant to an invention may not even be contemporaneous and therefore cannot be presented to the senses in any shorter period than their natural sequence requires. The process that extends through days or months cannot be perceived as a whole, but it may be reconstructed in the mind. We may run through the sequence in imagination as easily and rapidly as we may mentally review an extensive and intricate region of space. The plough is not a complicated implement if we consider merely its material shape; but its invention involved much more than the fortunate production of this geometrical form. It involved this form in relation to the materials of which it is made, the ground that it breaks, the seed time and harvest it makes possible. The mind that conceived it must have found room to represent the sequence as a whole, apart from which the curves of the ploughshare would have had no more meaning than an abstract sculpture.

Thus, besides the specific device to which the term *invention* is usually applied, there is also the situation—which may be complex and widely extended in space and time—to which the device is related. In the mind of the inventor—whatever may be the occasion of the final inspiration—the whole of this situation must be represented. Some part is, at the critical moment, represented by an actual experience: the overflowing bath, the swinging lamp, the falling apple, the twitching legs of a frog. But these trivial experiences are significant only to the mind already equipped with the complementary components of the discovery and capable of marshaling them.

External peirasis may lead to new conjunctions, and it will check and sometimes correct the false constructions of the mind. But it can never carry an animal very far beyond its customary range of achievement. Experiment must be local and brief, whereas the imagination can run over wider realms of space and time. By external peirasis we may discover a new recipe for jam but not a scheme for irrigating a desert. Our language suggests an illusory simplicity. We speak of looms and weaving as we speak of knives and cutting. But while chance may put a broken flint into a man's hand if he has the habit of picking up small objects, chance will not set up a loom for him. Nevertheless every element or ingredient with which the imagination works has been derived from some direct sensory experience gained in commerce with the concrete world. Experiment is the only process we can understand by which an animal can get to know its world. It begins with the blind groping of the protozoan, which probes its world by tentative excursions. Such mechanical exploration is elaborated by the development of new sense organs, but does not at first reach far into surrounding space, and scarcely at all into time. Eyes and ears and nose extend the range of passive experience but not the range of physical experiment. It is the memory that stores and the imagination that experimentally rearranges the successive patterns of experience, which make possible those composite and far-ranging explorations that yield human knowledge. Yet the mind can only direct and suggest; its experiments, though unlimited in scope, are made with uncertain materials, and its constructions must always be realized in concrete form before they can be tested.

At first, then, nature provided the tools and weapons, and man had merely to learn to use them skillfully and select them with understanding. Next he learned to improve the rude products of nature. This transition from the first stage of invention, when nature was ransacked for usable objects, to the later stage, when she was expected to supply only raw materials, is important for our purpose. For it is this change in man's manner of exploiting nature that produced one of the most conspicuous differences between human and animal invention.

Although we can all make discoveries and inventions of a sort, we do in fact learn most of our practice from instruction. The cumulative gains of human culture would not be conceivable otherwise. We think of instruction as chiefly verbal, but its basis is always imitation; even verbal communcation is based very largely on imitative behavior.[27] It is man's greatly developed skill in imitation that underlies the phenomena of human language and human culture. And yet to a great extent teaching must consist of practical demonstration. This limits the range of matters that can be handed on by tradition to practices that may be copied. Abstract knowledge of the external world, knowledge, that is to say, that is not directly related to some practical operation that can be visibly demonstrated, can only be transmitted by language. But language had to be invented and transmitted and could not serve as a medium for its own invention. Hence we must trace all human knowledge, abstract or otherwise, to the primitive modes of discovery common to ape and man, to the development of the human brain, and to the accumulation of achievements by tradition, depending on the processes of demonstration and imitation.

Invention is by no means always the daughter of necessity. Too much excitement or eagerness is unfavorable to the effective working of any mental process. The more urgent the need, the more likely is the animal to resort to external peirasis, like the cats and dogs in Thorndike's boxes. For reflection to have a chance there must be a state of comparative repose. The fact that invention comes more readily in the course of play activities than under the stress of real need is suggested by more than one of Köhler's experiments (play will therefore be the subject of a later chapter). But the discovery made during play can only be exploited if it is linked up in the brain with situations in which it can be utilized.

Let us look again at Köhler's experiments with chimpanzees. The tools commonly used by the chimps were hollow canes. On one occasion Sultan was given two such canes of about equal length, one of which was slender enough to be inserted into the hollow end of the other. Fruit was placed outside the bars and so far away that it could not be reached with the aid of a single cane. After some vain efforts with one cane Sultan let it fall outside the bars and used the second one to push the first toward the fruit. He succeeded in this way in touching and moving the fruit but could not, of course, draw it in. After a while Köhler tried to help him by poking one finger into the hole at the end of the larger cane. Sultan seemed to pay no attention to this movement and retired to sit on a box some distance away. Presently he got up, went and picked up both pieces of cane, returned to his box, sat down and began to play with them. While thus engaged in apparently aimless twiddling he happened to bring the two ends together in such a way that one entered the hole in the other. Immediately he darted to the bars—he had been sitting with his back half turned to them—and began to draw in the banana with the double cane. The canes fell apart, but he at once put them together again and accomplished his goal.

It does not seem likely that the hint given by Köhler counted for anything in this result, for he found that in general imitation played very little part in suggesting new methods to the chimps. The actual discovery that the two canes could be joined was evidently made by chance. The inventive act consisted in the realization that this possibility could be exploited. So long as Sultan's mind was mainly preoccupied with the fruit there was little probability of such a fortunate accident occurring. Even when it did occur, the accidental discovery would not have helped him if it had not been possible for the physical manipulatory experience to enter into combination with a representation in the brain of the situation in which it could be exploited. In this particular case the required tool was provided by an accidental manipulation; in another case it might be encountered ready-made in the course of perambulation. But in either case, if the chance event is to furnish an invention, the optical experience must be brought somehow into relation with the memory of a situation to which it is relevant. Of course, the accident may occur while the animal is actually trying to solve the problem. In that case success may be attributed to external peirasis, though even here it is possible to distinguish purely groping methods from experiments guided by reflection.

Köhler adds an epilogue to this account of Sultan and the two canes that is, perhaps, of even greater interest than the story of the discovery. The canes fit together rather too loosely, so that they easily fall apart, but Sultan puts them together again without any hesitation. Köhler comments:

> The operation seems to afford him immense pleasure; he seems to feel very lively, pulls all the fruit to the bars one after another without taking time to eat any, and, when I again separate the sticks, quickly putting them together begins to fetch in all kinds of indifferent objects from outside the bars.[28]

It is apparent that the means has become the end. Throughout the history of human invention we can observe the same process. The skill and ingenuity of the inventor afford him more pleasure than the profits of his invention. The tool first contrived in the service of some need becomes an end in itself. It would be hard to exaggerate the importance of this process in the history of the human mind.

10 *Mechanical Models, Symbols, and Mechanical Symbolism*

All animals make experiments, whether in the ordinary course of external peirasis under the impulse of some immediate need, or in play, or as the accidental result of some unexpected environmental circumstance. But man has learned the value of experimenting, and the practice of deliberate and controlled experimentation has led to the use of substitutes. The substitute is any material object or set of objects that may be operated upon instead of something else that is less accessible or less amenable to such operations. A simple model is the most obvious example. Models are used for communication and also in certain magical practices.[29] The extent to which they must resemble their prototype will depend on the use to which they are to be put. For magical operations, such as inflicting injuries or diseases in vital places, the model must be exact enough to show the external shape of the human body. For a dressmaker's dummy many details of form may be neglected. For the purpose of counting heads, no particular form is required at all. Maps and plans show the particular details required and neglect everything else. Working models of machines, if on a small scale, can never be exact. Details are omitted that are not indispensable for the end in view.

In all such cases the model, the plan, the map, the dummy are designed to be handled in some manner that corresponds to the normal handling of the prototype. But the small size and simplified form have two advantages. They allow experiments to be performed on a cheap substitute that can be more easily replaced if damaged or destroyed; and a greater number of experiments can be performed in a given time than on the real thing, where indeed many might be altogether impossible. We wish to divert a river, build a bridge, construct a ship, or dig a tunnel. We do not go to work at once on the site and put into operation the first plan that suggests itself. If we did it would in many cases be impossible to try a second. So we make some sort of dummy to represent the essential conditions of our problem and begin by experimenting with that. On a map we may make many experimental voyages less extensively and more rapidly than over the ground. Rearrangements of large and awkward objects may be tested out on a board with counters. Although small models are most often used in the design of larger objects, yet for certain purposes large models are required, as in the study of the behavior of minute and inaccessible things such as atoms and molecules, of which models are employed to illustrate crystal structure.

This substitute, which I shall call a *mechaneme,* is some physical object or apparatus on which we can make experiments, instead of experimenting directly on that part of our environment which really interests us. If the results of such experiments are to be of any value, there must exist a definite relation between the dummy and the real thing, which ensures that any conclusions drawn from experiments with the dummy shall be equally valid for application to the reality. But since the dummy must differ in many ways from the latter, being necessarily much simpler, this transferable validity can be ensured only if the conclusions on which we rely are derived exclusively from properties common to both model and reality. We make a pattern for a dress out of paper because we are concerned in our calculations only with the few characteristics of thinness, flexibility, and size common to the paper and the cloth. If we are concerned only with numbers and groupings, it may be permissible to represent the most complex objects by mere counters or strokes on paper. At first pebbles or strokes or sticks were used to represent other objects for the purpose of counting because, so far as relations of number are concerned, one set of things is as good as another, and for easy manipulation these simple handy objects are more convenient. Later, people realized that instead of using large numbers of pebbles, when recognizable grouping became impossible, one could take pebbles of different size or shape and make one kind equivalent to a certain number of another kind. This led to the invention of the abacus, where the counters have different values according to their position on the counting board. Mathematical tables can be regarded as an elaboration of the abacus.

The mechaneme is always some kind of physical apparatus that can be manipulated. Handling a mechaneme, therefore, is a form of external peirasis and does not differ from any other form of it except in the application of results. Since mechanemes provide a substitute for normal experimental behavior, their use resembles internal peirasis, for the ideas and memories with which we experiment are likewise a substitute for the real thing. But the difference is obvious. The mental substitute resembles the reality as closely as memory allows. Its imperfections are due to the limitations of experience and the uncertainty of memory. The physical substitute resembles the real original merely in certain particular features, but in these the resemblance is nearly perfect. If the mechaneme has been properly chosen or constructed discoveries may be made with its aid that could not be made otherwise.

In internal peirasis only rearrangements of past experiences are possible, and nothing entirely new, therefore, can result from it. The mechaneme is a material construction subject to physical laws like the real system it represents. So long as our experiments are concerned only with the consequences of such physical laws they cannot lead us astray. But our ideas are not subject to the same laws as the real phenomena they represent, and therefore the experiments we make with them are not to be relied on without continual checking. The value of internal peirasis consists mainly in its speed. Experiences that have taken long periods to acquire can be recapitulated in the memory very briefly, and yet sometimes quite effectively. We can in the imagination combine the results of several experiences. To combine them in fact would involve going through them all over again. In many cases we need to know the result of repeating an action many times. If the result is always the same, we need not perform the experiment but can repeat it in imagination to discover the cumulative result. This is a familiar experience to the mathematician. But the reliability of all such internal experiments is uncertain.

Operations with a mechaneme can, of course, be imagined like any other operation. And in some cases it may be advantageous to use the idea of the mechaneme in performing a piece of internal peirasis. This will happen only in special cases where the manipulations with the mechaneme are more familiar, or more easily remembered, than the operations for which they are a substitute. Here again mathematics furnishes the best example.

When we calculate mentally we are performing internally an experiment that could be performed in the concrete. But the addition of three to five can be performed in the concrete only by actually shifting three objects into proximity with five others. In our mental operations we may shift sheep as easily as counters, provided they are not too numerous. But we can picture to ourselves the counters arranged on the abacus much more clearly than a flock of moving sheep. And we can more easily picture to ourselves the act of shifting a counter on the board than that of driving a sheep into another pen.

The term *symbolism* is often used for the relation between a mechaneme and its real prototype. The use of this term has, however, given rise to confusion. I have referred elsewhere to the confusion between isolated symbols and symbolic *systems,*[30] and to the erroneous assumption that because words may be regarded as symbols of the things they denote, therefore language is a symbolic system like mathematics. The ordinary dictionary definition refers to the isolated symbol, as when white is said to symbolize purity, or the cross Christianity. "Belle Vue" may be the name of only one house in the street, and it may therefore be taken as an unambiguous symbol for that house. Every house in the street may have a name that symbolizes it in the same unambiguous way, but knowledge of these names will not tell us anything about the relative positions of the houses, as numbers can if they are assigned according to an intelligible system. The numbers form a system, which is more than a mere collection of disconnected symbols. Isolated symbols must be learned one at a time, and they can be used only as indicators. But systems of symbols serve another purpose, since we can perform experiments on them. By studying the figures and other symbols in a railway timetable one can discover what journeys may be undertaken and how long they will last. A system of coordinates is a more refined system of symbols than a mere set of numbers, since from the arithmetical relations between two sets of coordinates we can infer the geometrical relations between the two points. With a map and a timetable we can make experimental voyages and draw all kinds of useful conclusions about time, expense, fatigue, and other matters that the real voyages are likely to involve.

The symbolic system, therefore, resembles a mechaneme in that one can make substitute experiments on it which are then in their results transferable to a real situation. It differs in that it depends more on convention. In working on a model or other material mechaneme we rely on the physical character of the apparatus. In working with a symbolic system we depend in part on rules and conventions. If, in dressmaking, we first experiment with paper patterns, it is because we know that shapes that can be made out of paper can also be made out of cotton or silk. The laws of geometry apply to both, and we know that inferences drawn from an experiment on the paper will be valid also for the more costly material. But there is no such correspondence between a timetable and a railway system. The use of a timetable involves interpreting the conventions. The figures denote times and the columns the passage of a train from one station to another, and there is no simple correlation between the symbols employed and the movements of the trains.

Nevertheless this difference is not really fundamental. There are always conventions to be recognized in every mechaneme, and there is always some material structure in every system of symbols. The results of experiments performed on a model must always be interpreted, and in such interpretation there is always an element of convention. In a symbolic system no set of rules would suffice unless the symbols themselves were under some material restraint. A system of symbols must be such that, given a set of rules, definite consequences are deducible from them. But no deduction would be possible unless the symbols, by their own nature, in some way limited their own feasible arrangements. Every system of symbols must be composed of some kind of natural things—marks, counters, tokens, signs—and these are subject to natural law like everything else. The systems most often employed are written on paper, and are therefore arranged in a two-dimensional field; hence we cannot put them side by side in space as we might if we allowed ourselves three dimensions. What we can do with our symbols, therefore, is not independent of the practical means adopted for representing them. The combinations, permutations, and orientations of which they are susceptible are prescribed not only by convention but by the physical character of the medium in which they are constructed. A symbolic system is flexible, but only within certain limits, like a box of bricks. If the bricks had no mass, no shape, no persistent identity, then no structures could be formed from them at all.

The value of the set of symbols lies in the fact that the natural alterations or rearrangements to which it is subject correspond in some definite way to the natural changes in some other set of things, which is less easily manipulated or less easily explored, so that experiments and calculations may be carried out on the symbolic set that would be impracticable on the other. And yet all conclusions drawn from such vicarious experiments are applicable to both systems. Arbitrary sets of noises, shapes, or anything else may be chosen as symbols, and arbitrary operations and rules prescribed. But until it has been shown that such a system, in virtue of the rules laid down and of the physical nature of the symbols, can be correlated with some set of phenomena in nature, it cannot be regarded as a symbolic system. Such correlation can only be finally established by experiment.

In this sense of the expression, it is obvious that language is not a symbolic system. You cannot experiment with verbal formulas and utilize the experimental results as you can the results of experiments with bricks, geometrical drawings, or algebraic equations. Linguistic formulas serve rather for indexing purposes. The final results of complex operations with material objects can be recorded in the memory as statements, rules, or maxims. Such formulas as "acid corrodes metals," "horses eat oats," or "sugar dissolves in water," do not lend themselves to fruitful experiment. We can of course, like Molière's *maître de philosophie,* convert "acids corrode metals" into "metals are corroded by acids," or "by acids are metals corroded," or even "metals by acids corroded are." But most people might feel, as he did, that there was little profit in the changes. We certainly cannot find out anything about alkalies, however we juggle the formula, nor even anything further about acids or metals. But the phrase recalls a whole series of remembered experiments and serves to link them together in the memory.

By its power to evoke memories of material experiences, language fulfills its function of communication and record. It consists of a very large number of symbols, but they are so imperfectly organized into a system that they can only be used to suggest and never to represent. No symbolic system could, in any case, suffice to represent the whole of nature; yet there is no part of nature that is not included in the domain of linguistic expression. Words are labels that we commit to memory in association with ideas of any kind and of any degree of complexity. These ideas can be evoked by the use of the associated words, but only in minds in which the association has been established. There is no kind of correspondence between the nature and complexity of the idea and the form of the word. For every English-speaker the single syllable *I* symbolizes a complex of thoughts and memories he or she could never enumerate or analyze. And for every English-speaker it symbolizes an entirely different complex.

What distinguishes mathematics from other sciences is its elaborate symbolism. Some writers even appear to hold that it is exclusively concerned with this symbolism. Yet since the truths of mathematics may sometimes be equally well represented by alternative symbolic methods, it seems to follow that we should distinguish between the symbols and that which is symbolized. This, however, is not generally admitted. It is held that the mathematician is not concerned with any concrete aspect of nature but only with the properties of his own invention. This view may perhaps be accounted for as follows.

In the search for certainty and absolute truth philosophers have frequently turned to mathematics. Nothing seems less open to doubt than the proposition that two and two make four (and other similar mathematical propositions), and so the opinion has sometimes been expressed that whereas all other kinds of scientific truth are only "probable," those of mathematics are "certain." But how was this difference to be explained? One answer that has been given is that mathematical reasoning owes its infallibility to its exclusive dependence on deductions from arbitrary definitions. This implies that truth in mathematics means equivalence of symbols and has nothing to do with the natural world. Two and two make four, not because of anything prevailing in the universe at large, but just because mathematicians have decided to make it so.

Dugald Stewart, the Scottish philosopher who was a professor of mathematics and also the son of a mathematician, held for instance that in mathematical reasoning we are not seeking to establish relations between real phenomena but only to draw out the consequences of our own arbitrary ordinances. In this way he apparently not only established the certainty of mathematics but also denied its inductive basis. Hence, he referred with strong disapproval to James Ferguson's efforts to establish any geometrical theorems of which he had need by practical tests and by measurements with ruler and compass. Ferguson, a self-taught astronomer and laborer's son, invented special mechanical contrivances for his purposes, cutting, for instance, a card so as to afford ocular proof that the squares of the two sides of a right-angled triangle actually filled the same space as the square of the hypotenuse. Sir Thomas Heath (the British classical scholar and mathematician, 1861-1940) thought that Pythagoras himself may have arrived at his discovery by a similar method.[31] When Ferguson was sent, at the age of ten, to watch sheep, he mapped the heavens with the aid of his compasses and his homemade geometry, and later he constructed a clockwork planetarium. In due course he became a fellow of the Royal Society. But Stewart saw in Ferguson's methods only evidence of poor education (his schooling lasted only three months) and of "the early and exclusive hold which experimental science had taken of his mind," which disposed him to find "the refined and scrupulous logic of Euclid" tedious.[32] We may perhaps feel less sure that the educational advantages were all on the side of the professor of mathematics. If Stewart had been privileged to share the shepherd boy's observatory instead of sitting on a bench in his father's lecture room, it might have occurred to him that it was thus that geometry was discovered and not by the "refined and scrupulous" methods of Euclid and the Schools.

Now if mathematics really does symbolize something and is not merely an arbitrary system of ciphers and rules, if there does exist a set of natural facts which the symbols of the mathematician serve to represent, then we ought to be able to disentangle them from the symbols. The symbols used by the chemist serve to express natural facts, and there is no danger of confounding the properties of a substance with the structural formula that represents them. Where it is possible to make reliable deductions from the formula, or from a chemical equation, this is because the formula has been adapted to the facts. When experiment fails to confirm the deduction, the formula is altered or its implications are revised. It might even be possible, as Stewart suggests, to construct a system of chemical symbols for imaginary elements, together with arbitrary rules for their combination and arbitrarily assigned properties for the resulting compounds, but up to the present chemists appear to have shown little taste for this kind of recreation. Although they have conceived many systems, they have always claimed that these systems conformed to the facts of nature, and have sought to justify them on this ground. In the case of chemistry the danger of confounding facts with formulas is precluded by the existence of everyday terms. The familiar facts and aspects of chemistry have familiar names and can be described and discussed without the use of technicalities. The symbols are always recognizably a second (perhaps superior) method of describing phenomena which can be observed and described without their help. But the elementary facts of number and shape have become so closely associated with the symbols of arithmetic and geometry that both fact and symbol often enter the experience of the child together and are afterwards inseparable.

This, perhaps, accounts for Stewart's view. But more recently other circumstances have helped to confirm his view that the mathematical system has been constructed quite arbitrarily, and that it is little better than a stroke of fortune that it should have turned out as useful as it has. Such an opinion could not have arisen from the study of the history of mathematics, for this seems clearly to show the contrary. It is more probably due to the discovery in recent times that one may construct mechanemes, similar to those of conventional mathematics, with which calculations may be performed, although they appear to correspond to nothing in nature. Minkowski's geometry, invented without any practical design, was later found to admit of a practical application. If such systems, known to have been arbitrarily invented, are nevertheless found to have an unforeseen use, why should not arithmetic too have been an arbitrary invention, whose utility was only subsequently recognized?

It has also been pointed out that geometrical reasoning does not strictly apply to concrete things. Real triangles, if we may talk of such things, do not have three angles whose sum is precisely two right angles. The definitions of Euclid do not refer to anything in nature, yet all the reasonings of geometry are based on them. This is true, however, of all mechanemes, which are necessarily to some extent arbitrary and cannot correspond exactly with the realities on which they are modeled. All scientific definitions are open to the same objection. The zoological specification of a lobster is as abstract as the geometrician's definition of a circle. But just because of this we do not say there are no real lobsters. On the contrary, the meaning and justification of the definition rest on lobsters' existence and on nothing else. When we are thinking or reasoning about them, the zoologist's brief specification will often be more handy than a live lobster, although it is well to have a look at a real specimen from time to time. And so with mathematical abstractions. In practice we are concerned with circular objects; but for the purposes of thought and calculation a circle drawn on paper is more convenient than a millstone or a cartwheel. Very often a definition may be more useful still. Even here, however, it is wise to check our conclusions now and then by reference to real things.

But mathematics does not consist only of a system of abstract ideas and definitions. It also involves the "logical filiation," as Stewart calls it, "of consequences which follow from an assumed hypothesis." He says that if from our hypothesis we reason with correctness, nothing can be wanting to complete the evidence of the result. But how do we know that one consequence rather than another follows? If the definitions are arbitrary, why should not the inferences be arbitrary too? If the relation $2 + 2 = 4$ is arbitrarily established by definition, how can we deduce anything from it?

Two answers to this question have been suggested. Either something in the structure of the human mind inherited by all members of the race makes logical deductions from such propositions inevitable; or the mind comprises two fundamentally distinct faculties, one that learns by experience and another that knows by intuition, and some of the features of the universe are ascertainable by one faculty and others by the other.

Commenting on the first of these two answers: the fact that the mind of every animal has a definite structure and character that determines the broad features of its behavior will not be questioned by any zoologist, and the ways in which we think and believe are certainly determined by inherited mental characters. The psychological problem is to discover the nature of this determination, and we can do so only by the normal scientific methods of observation and experiment, both of which indicate quite clearly that there is no general characteristic of the human mind that makes logical deductions inevitable. In particular, it is only those who have a good deal of experience and practice with mathematical symbols to whom mathematical deductions of any but the most elementary kind appear even plausible. Thus the first of the two answers is unsatisfactory, and in consequence the second is usually adopted by philosophers.

What we have learned by experience, says the philosopher, we can never know to be universally true. However many times I have watched the tide come in, I can never be quite sure that it will come in again. If, then, I have an invincible conviction that 2 + 2 = 4 not only always has proved true but always will do so, as long as the universe endures and after, then I cannot have learned this from experience. I have therefore some other means of recognizing truth that does not depend on any process of learning by experience.

Now it will be seen that this does not really answer the question as it was stated on page 85. If the truths of mathematics are based on arbitrary definitions that have no relation to the real universe, except that they are products of the human imagination, then there seems no reason to suppose that this intuitive faculty for recognizing certain kinds of truth should have any jurisdiction where no truth is involved but only purely human conventions.

There are philosophers who believe that the fundamental principles of logic are directly evident to intuition. They then endeavor to deduce the principles of mathematics from them. Others have tried to show that the principles of logic are as much a matter of arbitrary definition as those of mathematics. A. J. Ayer (the British philosopher born in 1910) seems at one time to have held such a view. He wrote:

> The proposition that a material thing cannot be in two places at once . . . is not empirical at all, but linguistic. It simply records the fact that, as the result of certain verbal conventions, the proposition that two sense-contents occur in the same visual or tactual sense-field is incompatible with the proposition that they belong to the same material thing. And this is indeed a necessary fact. But . . . it is necessary only because we happen to use the relevant words in a particular way. There is no logical reason why we should not so alter our definitions that the sentence "A thing cannot be in two places at once" comes to express a self-contradiction instead of a necessary truth.[33]

Thus the principles of logic depend on the conventions of language. We do not ground the denial that a thing may be in more than one place at a time on any observation or experience but on the fact that our language has been made that way. We could as well have decreed that nothing may be in less than three or more than five places at once, and if our ancestors in their wisdom had so decided this would have become for us a self-evident proposition. It is really a piece of luck that our language should turn out to accord with vulgar experience. One might think that if the truths of logic and mathematics depended on nothing but human conventions they would not seem more, but rather less, evident than the truths we have been taught by experience. And it might seem a strange coincidence that so many different languages, so diverse in other ways, should have agreed to fix the same rule for the number of places in which a thing may be at the same time. But Ayer, when he wrote the preceding passage, evidently believed that such propositions as these were more difficult to disbelieve than empirical ones. In *Critique of Pure Reason* (1781) Kant called propositions that could not be doubted *apodeictic,* and Ayer uses the same word. He says:

> . . . there is nothing mysterious about the apodeictic certainty of logic and mathematics. Our knowledge that no observation can ever confute the proposition "7 + 5 = 12" depends simply on the fact that the symbolic expression "7 + 5" is synonymous with "12," just as our knowledge that every oculist is an eye-doctor depends on the fact that the symbol "eye-doctor" is synonymous with "oculist." And the same explanation holds for every other *a priori* truth.[34]

But why propositions based on linguistic conventions should be so impossible to disbelieve is not explained. Accordingly, the view of Stewart that mathematics is based on arbitrary definitions is not made any more acceptable by Ayer's extension of the theory to the principles of logic.

Some of the philosophical difficulties disappear when it is realized that mathematics is a symbolic system based originally on a collection of mechanemes. The fact that a mechaneme is an artificial construction does not mean that its appropriate manipulation cannot reveal any new truths that were not known before it could be constructed. On the contrary, it is the virtue and purpose of every mechaneme to facilitate experimentation. We experiment with the paper pattern for a dress more easily and more cheaply than with the cloth, and with figures on paper more easily than with bricks, tiles, or flagstones.

The mechaneme that was first developed to deal with numbers and shapes was later found to be useful for other purposes. This extension of the application of the primitive apparatus led to its modification and elaboration. Thus the number system used for reckoning for discrete objects was extended in order to be applied to processes and continuities. And this purposeful extension emphasized the artificial character of the mechaneme. In modern applications of mathematics to physics the distinction between symbols and physical facts is clear enough as a rule. But it is not always realized that the primitive symbols were a mechaneme in the same sense, and that they represented material facts in the same way that field equations represent the distribution of magnetic or electrical conditions or that a vector represents a velocity or a force.

11 *Origins of Mathematics*

The Abstraction of Number

Of the various "things" in which people find themselves interested, there are some that consist of groups of similar objects; and it may often be of importance to know whether such groups are intact or whether they have been increased or diminished. An alteration in number in such a case is just as likely to be a significant change, from the human point of view, as an alteration in shape, color, size, or movement. As we have seen in Chapter 5, the abstraction of a quality or characteristic is effected when an animal's reaction to an object possessing this quality is correlated with it exclusively. If, to a number of objects otherwise different, an animal behaves in the same way on account of their having the same color, smell, or shape, then its sensory and nervous apparatus can evidently pick this particular quality from the complex in which it is a component and adapt its reactions specifically to it. In order for such abstraction to occur, there must be some ground for it. The quality in question must be in some way independently related to the needs of the animal, so that experience and external peirasis may bring it constantly to the animal's attention. To understand the abstraction of number, therefore, we must show how this quality attracted attention as something separate, independent of all the other features by which objects or events were recognized.

In the first place there are objects made up of a number of similar parts. The design in Fig. 2 is, for us, obviously an arrangement of six similar parts, and even if the parts were less simple, as in Fig. 1, we should recognize the number as a constituent of the form. But we have been trained to detect numerical features and are inclined to rely on them for description and recognition. Nevertheless such figures can be recognized without such analysis. Animals learn to distinguish shapes and groups which, to our view, differ chiefly in the number of their components. Pavlov showed that a dog can distinguish ellipses of different eccentricity, and there is no reason why a dog should not equally learn to distinguish Fig. 2 from Fig. 5 or Fig. 6. To do so the animal would not have to count the parts. In sum, where a number of parts are always found in the same configuration, the total shape is more important than the number of the parts.

Abstraction of the numerical element, like other abstractions, must

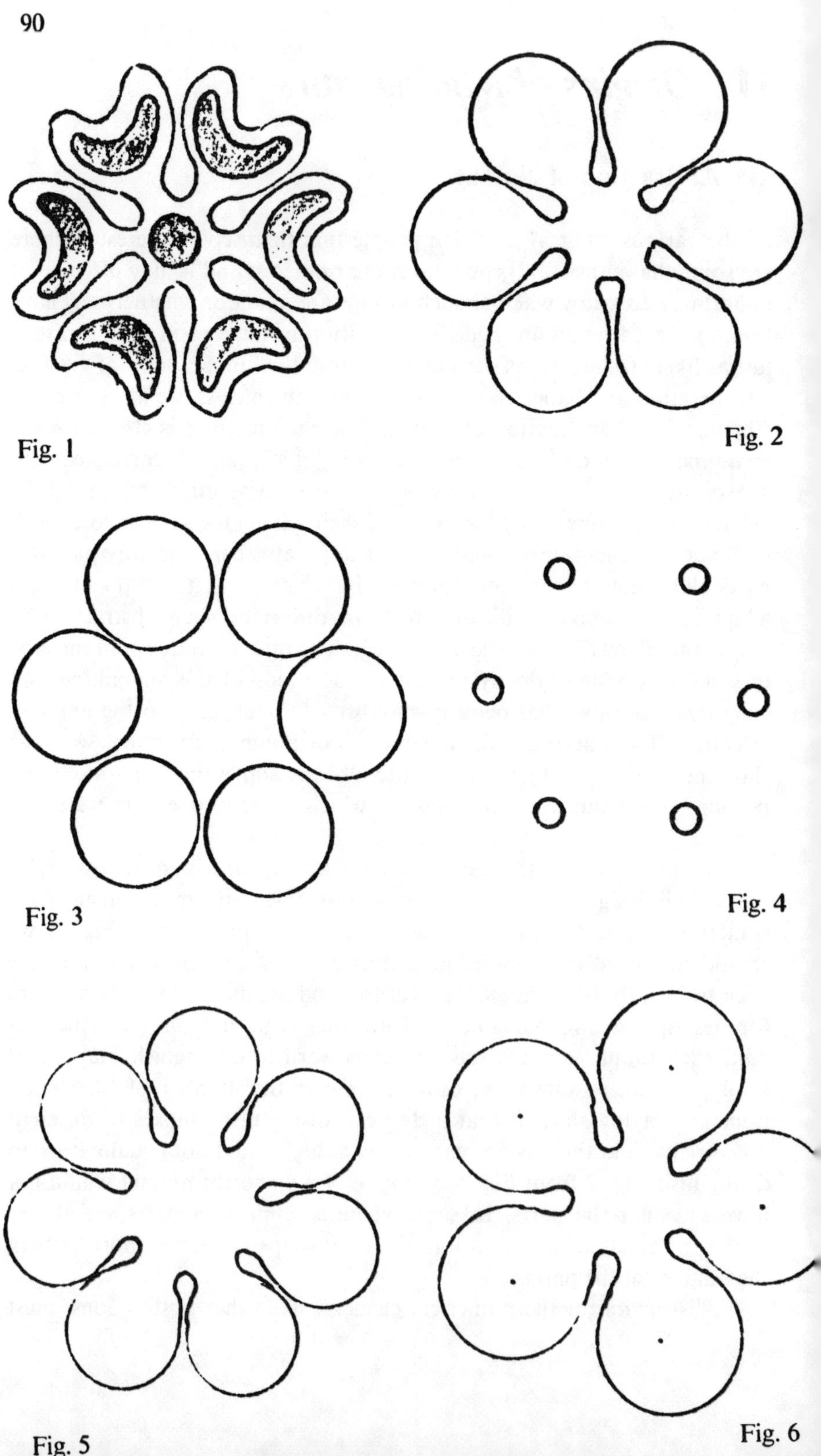
Fig. 1
Fig. 2
Fig. 3
Fig. 4
Fig. 5
Fig. 6

result from two kinds of experience: the comparison of different objects that have one characteristic in common and the comparison of similar objects that have one characteristic in which they differ. Figs. 1, 2, 3, and 4 are alike in two respects. Each consists of six similar parts, arranged in a circle. Thus they have a common numerical and a common geometric element. The latter is twofold and includes both the circular arrangement and the shape of the components. By varying the numerical element we encourage the abstraction of the geometric and vice versa. Figs. 2, 5, and 6 illustrate numerical variation combined with a constant geometric characteristic. But the separation of these two characteristics is not easy since the number of components is small, and consequently the difference in shape that results from the addition or subtraction of a single component is conspicuous and may be compared in degree with any other difference in shape not involving a numerical element. On the other hand, when the number of components is large, addition or subtraction of a few will not appreciably change the form, and so analysis of this latter will not be prompted.

In all the figures so far, there is no doubt as to what constitutes the component. But in more complex ones this may be less obvious. The practice of description, which played a large part in facilitating these abstractions, is much aided by a suitable selection of components which, by their number and arrangement, constitute the character of the whole. Even in a figure composed of very simple elements, it may be hard to see the complex as composite if they are not arranged symmetrically. Fig. 7 (p. 92) is made up of seven T-shaped elements, but that fact is not immediately evident; the shape of the whole could be represented mentally and remembered without such analysis. In Fig. 9 the composition is more striking.

Apart from objects such as flowers, where the numerical element is accompanied and to some extent masked by a geometric one, there also exist significant groups of *separate* objects that may be arranged in various configurations without any change in their number; and here the geometric element is lacking, or at least is variable. If a five-petaled flower or a six-legged animal is known by its form, then a missing petal or a missing leg may be noticed at once without any need for counting. But a litter of five kittens or a herd of five cows is not so easily recognized or distinguished from a group of only four. It is true they may be arranged in a recognizable formation and thus temporarily acquire a geometric character; but they do not naturally arrange themselves in this fashion, and it may not be easy to impose such an arrangement on them.

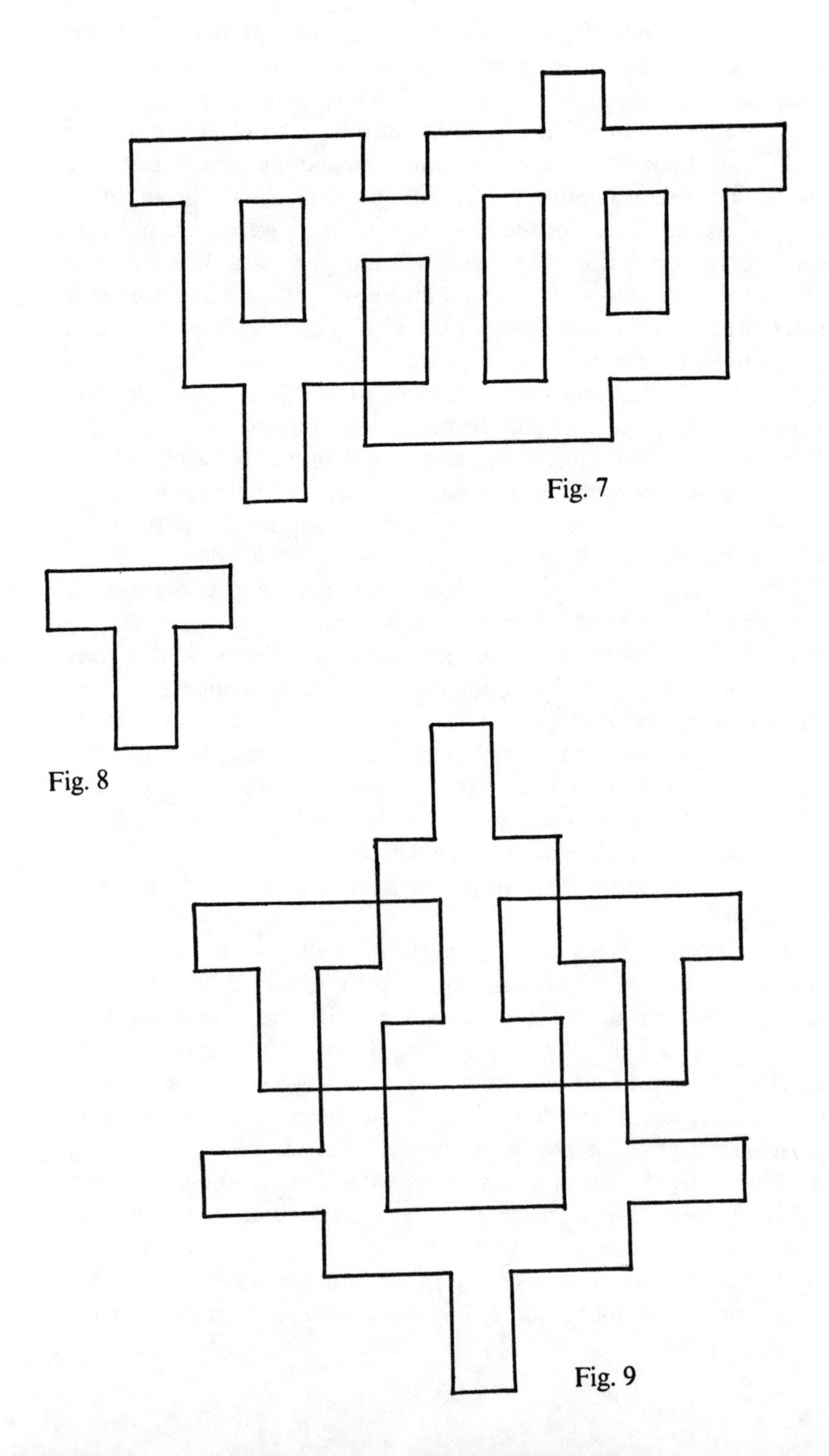

Fig. 7

Fig. 8

Fig. 9

We get over the difficulty by counting, but this is a sophisticated procedure that had to be invented.

If the objects are small and movable (but not able to move themselves), the simplest way to make sure that the group is intact is to arrange them in some known formation; for example, a group of three as an equilateral triangle, of four as a square, of five as a square with one in the middle, and so on, or like the pips on playing cards. In this way shape replaces number. Whenever it is necessary to check the group it must be rearranged; and the method is not available with large objects or objects that cannot be moved. It serves, however, for fairly large numbers, since small groups may be arranged in groups of groups. The experience of taking things to pieces and putting them together again also shows us that a group of movable objects may be recognized as intact if it can be arranged in a known configuration. When we have taken the clock to pieces, we may arrange the parts according to a conventional pattern, spread out on a sheet of paper. If we know the pattern we can see at a glance whether anything is missing. No counting is involved.

Knowledge that a group of objects may be arranged in a particular way serves then to check the group, but it does not imply any real abstraction of number. We may easily suppose that a dog would learn to distinguish the five of hearts from the seven—he would not, of course, thereby acquire any kind of understanding of the relation between five and seven—but it would be difficult to devise an experiment to test the dog's power of discriminating a group of five sticks from a group of seven. My dog will carry up to five small sticks, if she cannot find a large one, and is especially inclined to do so if she has been carrying a long one that has got broken, as she does not like to leave any of the pieces behind. If they become a little scattered when she puts them down for a few moments while she is exploring, she seems, when she returns to them, to know whether she has gathered up the whole bundle. But the feel of them in her mouth, their weight, and the gape of her jaws, may all suffice to tell her that one is missing. Many experiments have been made to ascertain whether and how far animals can count; but it is hard to exclude all other modes of recognition. Shape, weight, bulk may all serve this purpose without any reference to number. As long as it is only necessary to distinguish or to recognize groups of objects that can be *manipulated,* number is not necessarily involved.

The same number of objects admits of more than one arrangement. If we take account of small differences, the number of possible arrangements of a given set becomes indefinite. But there are certain arrangements—for example, such as can be made in one plane or have some obvious symmetry—which are easier to retain in the memory and to recognize. The simple experiment of exposing to view a group of black dots on a white ground for a short time shows that some groupings are more easily recognized than others. The fact that different patterns are equivalent must sooner or later come to light and lead to the establishment of various correspondences. Such discoveries are made by every individual at some stage in his life, but as his acquaintance with number grows, he becomes sophisticated and finds it hard to realize that such things were ever anything but self-evident. In a more primitive state of cultural development these experimental facts were not obvious.

The comparison of configurations will at first have established only the fact that there was a certain quality about a group that was independent of the way that its components were arranged. The study of such groupings, as well as experiments with pebbles and other counters, would gradually reveal the relations between different numbers; it is these which give rise to the mathematical operations of addition and multiplication. We think of numbers now as a closely related set, and were taught to count before we had much experience of real numerical situations. Five, six, and seven were associated together in a verbal sequence before any of them was connected closely with any tangible group or figure. Hence it is not easy for us to imagine a state of mind in which threeness, fiveness, or sevenness were represented in the mind and recognized as characteristics of real things, without any attention being paid to their relations to one another. Nevertheless this characteristic of numbers—that they can be combined to produce other numbers—had to be discovered, like the composition of colors and the laws of musical harmony.

These discoveries—that many different configurations were numerically equivalent and that particular numbers could be compounded out of other numbers—would gradually reveal the truth that the numerical character that had been abstracted from so many different experiences was quite independent of any of the shapes or configurations with which it had first been associated, and that any particular set of durable objects, if protected against destruction or loss, retained this character unaltered.

One consequence of this discovery was that it made possible the invention of the tally. By this I mean merely a set of convenient articles of known number that could be applied as a standard to determine the numerical extent of any other group, as a yardstick, meter, or gauge is applied to determine the length, weight, pressure, or any other quality of a thing. This use of the tally is based on the assumption, of course, that two sets must have the same number of components if they can be made to coincide. If I have just enough cups to match my stock of saucers, then I have the same number of each. Yet we cannot say that anybody discovered this, for such experiences were the very source and ground for the conception of numerical equality. Every time a party of men lay down their weapons together there is formed a pile that may be beyond the arithmetical resources of any individual to count. Yet when the same men return to take up their weapons, it will at once appear if one is missing or if one is left over. Such experiences, daily repeated with different articles and different numbers, illustrate and drive home the principle that sets of the most diverse objects may be compared in this way and that the congruence, once established, may be relied upon to persist, in whatever way the objects may be rearranged.

It seems reasonable to suppose that configuration would be the first mark by which a group was recognized. An isolated group of trees, a cluster of conspicuous mountain peaks, a converging system of tributaries, could be compared to the human hand primarily for the general similarity of shape; yet underlying the geometric comparison would be an implied numerical one, since a similar group of four or three would fail to sustain the comparison. The next step toward abstraction involves the two processes I have described: recognition that a group of movable objects is intact if it can be arranged in a known configuration, and use of the tally. It is especially in cases where the objects are not to be manipulated and do not allow themselves to be arranged in a particular pattern that the tally is required.

With the development of the various methods of communication (first self-explanatory gestures and later conventional signs), man needed names or signs for numbers, or rather for some of these specific numerical characters. Perhaps we must assume that some kind of conception of threeness, fourness, and fiveness must have preceded the invention of words or signs for these numbers. But we find in many languages of the more primitive peoples that the names for the smaller numbers are borrowed from the names of familiar objects that possess that particular numerical character; this suggests that the ideas were closely linked to that of shape. Not only the hand, foot, eyes, and arms served for this purpose. The British anthropologist E. B. Tylor (1832-1917), quoting Wilhelm von Humboldt, records that ages ago the scholars of India, selecting a set of words for a *memoria technica* in order to record dates and numbers, chose *moon* or *earth* to express one, there being but one of each.[35] Two might be called *eye, wing, arm,* or *jaw;* and four *veda, age,* or *ocean* (there being four of each recognized); and so on. Humboldt suggested that this late and sophisticated example illustrates a principle employed much earlier. "Indisputably," he said, "there lie at the root of all numerals such metaphors as these, though they cannot always be now traced." The name may be taken from an object, like the hand, which has a characteristic number of parts, or from a set of related things like the vowels or the signs of the zodiac. In the Indian case it is obvious that the names were used to denote abstract numbers; but in really primitive cases the comparison with objects of the first type, as hands, may rest on other characteristics beside the numerical one. Even so, the comparison—however it arose in the first instance—would tend to draw attention to the numerical element and so aid the abstraction.

There is, of course, nothing very peculiar in this manner of naming the numbers; in fact, it is not easy to think of an alternative method. All kinds of qualities are named in the same manner, by comparison with objects specially so characterized. Before the existence of words, the objects themselves would be utilized to suggest the qualities. We still employ the method and use familiar objects like pears, mushrooms, hearts, eggs, and kidneys to suggest certain shapes; oranges, blood, the sea, and the sky to suggest certain colors; feet, fingers, and steps to denote lengths; and for tastes and smells we have hardly any words that are not borrowed from familiar objects. To indicate number, as soon as names were required, there was no other method.

I have already noted that the ability to recognize a common character of threeness in two or more sets of objects, and of fiveness in other sets, does not imply any appreciation of the relation between the number three and the number five, any more than ability to recognize a circle and an ellipse and to distinguish one from the other implies an appreciation of their relationship and of the fact that they are but two members of an indefinite series of related entities. But the manipulation of counters and other movable objects and their arrangement into particular configurations for purposes of checking would eventually reveal the fact that, for example, two triangular arrangements could be combined to make a hexagonal one. From such experiences, continually repeated, would arise the recognition of the identities: two and three make five, three and four make seven, and so on. But even the accumulation of several such empirical formulas would not necessarily suggest the number *series;* and without the recognition of this unique series there can be no counting. Checking with a tally is not, of course, the same as counting. The use of the tally rests on the belief that the numerical character of any group of movable objects is independent of their momentary arrangement and is the same as that of any other set of objects that can be placed alongside them. It does not presuppose any special relation between one numerical character and another nor the knowledge that these numerical characters may be arranged in a particular order, fixed by the numbers themselves, and such that when they are so arranged none can be missing. This character of the natural numbers has been found to be possessed also by other mathematical assemblages. It had first to be discovered in the natural numbers themselves.

It seems as if the naming of the numbers was the first condition for this discovery. By naming we need not understand only the assignment of arbitrary sounds. If any numbers were represented at an earlier time by signs or gestures or marks we may suppose that these would be more closely related to the configurational character than sounds can be. Two strokes or two representations of any particular object would be the natural method of representing the character 2, especially in connection with particular objects. Even in the Egyptian hieroglyphic system this method of expressing a number of objects is sometimes employed. But whether gestures, sounds, or drawings were employed, so long as only a few numbers were required there would be no need for the construction of a series. An extension of the range would, however, lead to the adoption of systems calculated to aid the memory. Arbitrary names or signs, however skillfully chosen from objects that were suitably suggestive, could not be extended indefinitely, and of course they could not of themselves imply anything as to the relation between one number and another. The words *six* and *seven* may conceivably have once been the names of characteristic objects or groupings that suggested numbers, but in the names there is nothing to show that the number seven can be obtained from six by the addition of one. Even when this much had been realized, there is no reason why anybody should immediately see that by a repetition of this operation it would be possible to generate the whole series of natural numbers, and on this basis define—as Henri Poincaré undertook to do—the operation of addition.

When, however, a few number names had been adopted, certain combinations would be possible on the ground of concrete experiments. We find in many languages both addition and multiplication compounds, like *dix-neuf* and *quatre-vingts.* Tylor, writing of the Australian aborigines, notes that the Watchandie names for three and four are *two-one* and *two-two* respectively. In the Kamilaroi dialect there is an independent word for three, so that four, five, and six are *two-two, two-three,* and *three-three.* He adds that although a tribe may have no current words for numbers above three or five or so, they can count considerably further by falling back on what he calls "a lower and ruder method of expression than speech—the gesture-language."[36] What may have been a ruder method of *expression* may, however, have been a much more efficient calculus; and in fact we have here not a falling back on a ruder method but rather the specialization of an older form of communication for a new purpose. The names or signs that may have been convenient for simple record and communication were not suitable for use as a mechaneme.

Although number names did not lend themselves to calculations, they could be used quite effectively as a tally. If any list of words has been committed to memory so that it may be repeated by rote, it will serve this purpose as well as a string of beads. Tylor tells of a little girl who counted cards "January, February, March, April," and so forth, and adds that the numerical value of the Hebrew letters "is given with reference to their place in the alphabet, which was arranged for reasons that can hardly have had anything to do with arithmetic."[37] The letters of the alphabet were used by the Greeks in the same way, and a similar system was used by the Arabs.[38] As children we had a method of drawing lots that consisted in repeating a string of words and phrases *(Eena deena dinah do, catch a nigger by his toe . . .),* assigning each accented word to one of the competitors, and so continuing until the rigmarole came to an end. Since there were nineteen syllables in the counting rhyme, it would have been quicker to divide nineteen by the number of persons. But I do not believe we ever thought of the matter as a form of counting. We never inquired how many beads there were in this verbal tally; we told them off parrotlike without reflection.

Any sequence of this kind, once committed to memory, is always available and does not require any physical manipulation. One by one the words are checked off against the objects, and the last word checked is the name of the number of articles. By this means the equality of several different sets may be established. But while one arrives at the total number of a set of things, one does not learn anything about the composition of the number—that it is to say, about its relation to other numbers. We can use it to add, where we have tangible objects to deal with, since we put the groups together and add the whole by simple checking; but without such tangible objects it is not so easy to find the sum of two numbers. Combined with a set of counters, of course, it is more valuable. If I have a bag of a hundred pebbles, this will enable me to check a flock of a hundred sheep, but not a flock of sixty-seven unless I know beforehand that for this purpose I must first withdraw thirty-three from the bag. This implies a knowledge of the relations between numbers that is not essential for the simple use of the tally.

A further drawback lay in the limitation of memory. One cannot learn an indefinitely long sequence of words. Later, of course, by elaborating the system of using compounds, whether addition or multiplication compounds, a method of forming the number names by rule was introduced, which made it unnecessary to rely on a mere effort of memory. But for large numbers a tally of this kind soon loses its utility. One way—and perhaps the most obvious way—in which the use of a tally may lead to a better understanding of the relations between different numbers and so to what we may call true counting, is where the tally itself is short and has to be applied again and again, and a second tally is used to check the repetitions. When fingers and toes are used as a tally this method is often used; it underlies all later systems of numeration.

The Abstraction of Shape

The empirical origin of geometry is more generally recognized than that of arithmetic. The abstract geometry of the Greeks must have been preceded by some more practical kind of inquiry. It seems probable that it was mainly in connection with manufacturing activities and the division of land that men learned the importance of measurement, and that it was the methods and materials imposed on them by circumstances which drew their attention to the properties of straight lines, angles, and circles. In the construction of clothes and utensils, tools and dwellings, men and women found themselves faced with problems of shape and size; it was in the course of such activities that they discovered the virtues of those geometric characters. But before there could be geometry, there must have been a still earlier process of abstraction by which the forms of things came to be recognized as having a significance apart from the things themselves.

Objects, separated from the general situation, are recognized by their smell, sound, shape, and so forth. The smell or cry of a cat is often enough to enable a dog to recognize it. The smell and the sound are, as it were, automatically abstracted by the special senses to which they appeal. The visual appearance of an object may be abstracted in the same way, but shape and size and color and movement are all intermingled; the shape alone usually affects the retina quite differently according to the aspect represented. The momentary aspect is only one of the innumerable possible projections, and the real shape can be found only by exploration. It is thus very hard for the shape of an object to affect an animal independently of its color, its size, its position, and its movements, so long as the animal is dependent upon vision. It is of course not only with their eyes that animals recognize the shape of things. We saw that many lower creatures depend on their antennae, palps, and other movable appendages (p. 9). Even in the human the fingers are often the first tutors of the eye. The object grasped in the hands or embraced by the body presents a tactile image that depends on the posture and movements of the grasping organs.

The ability to recognize a thing by sight or by touch does not constitute the power of abstraction with which we are concerned. Abstraction of a quality or property means that the animal has learned to react to it to some extent regardless of other accompanying qualities. If it is merely recognized as the sign of a particular object, even though at the time no other quality is perceived, there is not necessarily any abstraction. Abstraction presupposes some constant response to the quality in a number of different contexts and a number of different things, so that it is the quality itself that is of interest and not the object of which it happens to be the signal.

It seems unlikely that we shall find any abstraction of shape except among humans, for it is hard to see how such a character can be of interest to other creatures apart from the object that bears the shape. The only case where this seems likely to occur is among tool-using animals like the chimpanzee. When the ape looks for a stick with which to reach some inaccessible object, we have seen (p. 45) that he will sometimes take a number of quite different objects because they appear to be of the required shape. Insofar as he can carry in his mind a specification of the desired object that is limited to or primarily consists of a particular shape, then we may say that he has accomplished one degree of abstraction. The nest-building animal that seeks materials of a particular shape, without regard to color, weight, or smell, has likewise taken the first step.

The fact that the only nonhuman examples that suggest themselves are concerned with the use of tools or the exploitation of materials for construction leads us to conjecture that it is man's creative activities—his manufacture of tools, weapons, clothes, and utensils—that have led him to pay special attention to the *shapes* of things, apart from their other qualities. It is often the shape that makes them appropriate for his purpose; and objects of different materials, obtained from different sources by the use of different methods, may, in virtue of their common shape, serve one and the same purpose. A simple illustration of this would be the use of stone, bone, and wood for the manufacture of piercing and cutting tools. Any endeavor to fashion a particular tool into the likeness of another that has been found serviceable would concentrate attention upon details of shape.

Still more important, perhaps, would be the recognition of suggestively shaped stones or rocks. At first the stone might be merely mistaken for the object it resembled, an error that can occur with other animals. Any animal but man would lose interest as soon as the error had been recognized. Somehow, as I have pointed out elsewhere, man found significance in such resemblances, even tried to improve them, and eventually learned to make models and images himself.[39] This practice more than any other would depend upon and encourage the process of abstraction, the ability to think of the form of an object apart from all its other qualities.

We may compare this first step in the abstraction of shape with that in the abstraction of number, which consisted in the recognition that groups of things are characterized by a certain property we now call number, which is independent of the arrangement and which may be common to two or more groups. The next step in regard to number was the recognition that this numerical property could be compounded, and that the numbers formed a system of members related to one another very closely, capable of being arranged in a unique order and of being combined by the processes of addition, multiplication, and so on.

In regard to shape we may see the next step in the analysis of complex shapes into simpler components, and the arbitrary composition of the latter to form new shapes. Such analysis can arise only from the comparison of similar shapes; it is in the deliberate construction of images or other objects in imitation of a given model that such a comparison is made necessary. Groups of objects may be compared by setting the members of one group alongside the members of the other, and simple shapes may likewise be directly compared, either by superposing flat objects so that their outlines coincide or (if the objects have straight edges) by bringing these together for a comparison of length. But in general one curved or irregular surface cannot be tested in the same way against another. This difficulty is overcome by the use of special measuring instruments designed to be applied to particular aspects of solid bodies—rulers, measuring tapes, calipers. Of course, these instruments in the form that we know them were designed with a full appreciation of the requirements they had to fulfill. The earliest instruments of this kind must have preceded such appreciation, and their use helped to determine the way in which shape was analyzed into lines, surfaces, curves, and angles. These were the aspects that could be measured; it was in the act of measuring them that the worker recognized their existence and so came to *abstract* them from the more complex forms in which they were naturally incorporated.

I have assumed that the earliest interest would be in like objects and in the manufacture of one object in imitation of another, so that the aim of measurement would primarily be to ascertain agreement and not to measure disagreement. When two objects can be directly compared—as, for example, two spears or arrows in respect of length or thickness—there is no need for a yardstick or common measure. But it surely did not escape early workers' notice that in making a large number of objects on the same model an error may accumulate if each new specimen is compared with the one just made, and that it is safer to keep one particular specimen as model for comparison with all the rest. In cases where direct comparison is not possible the need for a standard yardstick would assert itself. If equality was all that was required, the standard could be chosen afresh for each occasion. Only when a similar operation had to be repeated at different times and places would the need for a permanent standard arise. We know that almost everywhere the dimensions of the human body served as the first standards of length. When a fixed standard of this kind has been adopted (since the objects that have to be compared are of all possible lengths), it becomes necessary to take account of multiples and fractions of the standard; thus the idea of proportion came into existence. Nowadays we naturally express a proportion by means of a fraction—that is to say, by two numbers. But Euclid defines proportion without introducing the idea of number, at least expressly. It hardly seems probable, however, that before the development of Greek abstract geometry any clear idea of relation in size could dispense with the use of numbers.

The final stage in the abstraction of shape was reached when philosophers came to speak in the most general terms of the antithesis between form and matter. But the geometrician is not concerned with mere form in itself but with the analysis of particular forms into common elements and with the determination of the relations of different forms. In his investigations he finds it convenient, and indeed necessary, to substitute drawings and models for the real objects that are of primary interest; these drawings constitute the geometric mechanemes.

To recapitulate: The abstraction of shape, like other abstractions, results from the recognition of likeness amid difference. Two objects must be seen to be alike in shape, although different in other respects. This can happen only when the shape itself is of interest apart from the object it characterizes. Such interest is rare among other animals—if it occurs at all. In man it appears first in relation to accidental resemblances between natural objects of entirely different natures, as stones and animals. It is increased by the practice of making models and drawings, and still more by the manufacture of tools and other articles. When objects of the same form, serving the same purpose, are made from different materials, it is clear that an abstraction of shape has been achieved. The next step consists in an analysis of complex shapes into simpler components; this analysis leads to and is guided by the process of measurement, which at first consists merely in methods of comparison that are introduced where direct juxtaposition or even superposition is not possible. The use of fixed standards, which are required to ensure continuity in work at different times or places or by different craftsmen, leads to the idea of multiples and fractions and so to measurement in the general sense in which we understand it now. The craftsman's or the architect's need for planning resulted in a specialization of picture writing as a mechaneme, and the experiments in design made in this way led in time to the more abstract geometric investigations.

In view of the great influence geometry has had on the development of mathematics in general, it is of special interest to note its empirical basis, and also to see how it consists essentially in the exploitation of a mechaneme.

In conclusion: The thesis of this chapter and of the preceding one can be stated briefly in the proposition that mathematics originated as a mechaneme. At first pebbles or strokes or sticks were used to represent other objects for the purpose of counting, and this, as we saw, led to the invention of various kinds of abacus. On the other hand, the use of marks—that is to say, written strokes or strokes drawn on a clay tablet or a sand table—lent itself more readily to a variation of form with corresponding variation of meaning. Instead of two, three, or four strokes, single signs of peculiar shape were employed.

At the same time, in dealing with the shapes of things it was found that the real object could for purposes of measurement be replaced by a drawing, and out of the practice of reasoning about the dimensions of such substitutes there grew the science of geometry.

The next step was to bring these two mechanemes into relation with one another. This was achieved in two ways. On the one hand geometric constructions were used to solve arithmetical problems in the manner described by Sir Thomas Heath as "geometrical algebra." On the other hand arithmetical methods of measurement were applied to geometric problems. Before this latter application could be fully developed, algebra needed to be invented. Algebra was developed out of arithmetic by the gradual substitution of symbols of more general meaning. The use of letters instead of figures made it possible to concentrate attention on the relations between numbers without regard to the properties of any particular numbers.

From these developments came a written mechaneme that could be manipulated with less physical exertion than the abacus but which could assist in solving far more complex problems. Insofar as the manipulations of this new mechaneme could be mentally represented, it became available for internal peirasis. But this was always secondary. The great value of the new symbols lay in the fact that they could be subjected to the most complicated and protracted manipulations, far beyond what could be conducted in the imagination, and they were as reliable as the abacus if the manipulations were performed according to rule.

Many current misconceptions about language and mathematics seem to have arisen on the one hand from a failure to recognize in the latter this character of a mechaneme, and on the other from the unjustified attribution of that character to language. Perhaps both these misconceptions are due to the fact that the nature of the mechaneme has not been understood, and hence the importance of the part it plays in all scientific investigations has been generally overlooked. It is possible that a similar failure to appreciate the nature of the theoretical model has prevented psychologists from seeing the essential similarity between the conceptions of science and the notions of the primitive magician. I shall discuss the theoretical model in the following chapter.

12 *The Theoretical Model*

What the mechaneme is for external peirasis, the theoretical or conceptual model is, in a certain manner, for internal peirasis. It consists in the use of one familiar group or system of phenomena as a model for the explanation of another that is less well-known. Relief is afforded from the arduous description of a set of facts when it is possible to say that a certain fact *A* resembles in many or even all respects another fact *B*, which is already familiar—as when we say that the moon behaves like a heavy body in relation to the earth or that light behaves like a wave motion. Ernst Mach notes that such a theoretical model can enrich the fact or process we are investigating by suggesting that it may include characteristics "which we are now for the first time prompted to look for, and which we very often find."[40]

It is of course this fertility of certain hypotheses that makes them valuable to the scientist. They are not always fertile, and if we wish to understand the psychological foundation of this type of thinking, it is necessary to take into account the barren as well as the fruitful theories. The psychological foundation is briefly this: we must interpret new experiences in terms of the old. We must try to relate our passing sensations to our stock of ideas, interpreting the sounds, colors, forms, or smells recorded by our senses as things or events in space and time. Where the experiences of the moment are checked or interpreted against the stock of past experience there must be comparison. The simplest case of perception involves a comparison of immediate with past sensations in order to evoke the appropriate idea.

The comparison may lead to a more or to a less complete identification, and in normal perception the identification is complete. Sensations are interpreted as indicating the presence of a horse because they resemble sensations often before found to have that meaning. But a comparison may result in a merely partial identification. None of our ideas may fit the new experience exactly. A new animal or bird is discovered that does not exactly resemble any that has been seen before. But it bears a closer resemblance to some known species than to others, and from this partial resemblance its general features and habits may be to some extent predicted. Because we find nothing in our memory that corresponds *exactly* to the new phenomenon, we are not therefore deterred from applying our knowledge of *similar* phenomena. If this were not the case we should seldom be in a position to deal appropriately with any situation, since every situation is apt to have some novel features. When a cat is introduced to a small animal, such as a young guinea pig, she will behave toward it in one of her normal ways. She may adopt it as though it were a kitten, attack it as though it were a rat, or shrink from it in fear as from a hedgehog. This is merely the Pavlovian principle of generalization, according to which we respond to a new stimulus as if it were identical with another that merely resembles it in certain respects. A similar situation may, then, suffice to evoke the same reaction, and the similarity need not be at all close.

Pavlov also shows that further experience narrows the range of situations, so that the response no longer occurs in the case of situations outside a certain range of variation. The phase of generalization is followed by a phase of concentration, experience compelling us to make the distinction that we do not make at first (see p. 34). But if the practical effects of a wrong interpretation do not compel this rectification, we may continue indefinitely in the belief that things are the same although they have, in fact, very little in common. The primitive philosopher compared the eclipse of the moon to the swallowing of an object by an animal, supposing that the moon was devoured by a dragon. The French Egyptologist G. Maspero (1846-1916) notes that the ancient Egyptians believed the sky was stretched over the earth like an iron ceiling, supported by four forked trunks of trees, such as were used in the primitive house.[41] The same Egyptians also believed that the Nile flood was due to a tear dropped by Isis. In all these cases the less easily explicable phenomenon was compared to a familiar one. Such explanations had little or no practical value, since very little could be deduced from them, and for that reason such theories went unchallenged for a long time.

The desire for an explanation is not always based on any practical need. Very often it serves only the purpose of reassuring us and so dispensing with the need for any action. Many theories may be regarded less as tools to be applied for practical purposes than as tranquilizers. But the intellectual process involved in the formation of a theory is much the same in both cases, and only the tests are different. In the one case the test is in the practical application, in the other in its sedative effect (see p. 54). The extension and correction, of which Mach speaks, results from experiment in the case of the practical theory. If it occurs at all in the other case it will only be because of contradictions between rival theories. There is a certain need for consistency that sometimes leads to the modification of incompatible theories. Some such theoretical incompatibility may have led to the revision of the Egyptian theory about the sky.

When it was discovered that neither Bâkhû nor Manû were the limits of the world, it was necessary to withdraw the pillars of the celestial roof from sight, and imagine fabulous peaks, invested with familiar names.

All satisfactory explanations, whether of the practical or the reassuring kind, must be given in terms of what is understood, or at least of what is familiar and accepted as understood. The most direct form of explanation is simply interpolation or extrapolation, and this is, from the psychological point of view, extended perception. By supplying from our imagination the unperceived phases or aspects of an event, we recognize it as something familiar. In this way we explain to ourselves the particular aspect we happen to have seen or heard. A sudden noise is explained when it is shown that it was one aspect of a familiar occurrence, such as the dropping of a saucepan, the backfiring of a motor, or a distant storm. We discover the fallen saucepan and the cat that dislodged it. The additional facts may be disclosed by exploration, as in this case, or they may be merely imagined. Robinson Crusoe explained the footprint in the sand by supposing that there was another human being on his island. We explain the presence of fossils in the chalk by supposing that living creatures once perished in an ancient sea. In such cases we infer the unobserved and unobservable from what we actually see and investigate; and we base this inference on our experience of the normal sequence of things, without imagining anything different from common experience.

In the case of the theoretical model, although the model is conceived in some familiar form, yet it is applied with some special modification. In no man's experience could the shedding of a tear have had any effect on the rising of a river. But if we imagine some being large enough and sufficiently moved by grief, then the flow of tears might have such prodigious results. The explanation is of the same kind as in the case of the footprint in the sand, except that the imaginary agent has to be enormously magnified. In later times the more fruitful models were found to be micromodels—that is to say, the familiar events or processes supplied by the imagination had to be reduced to much less than their natural dimensions. Thus the various forms of atomic hypotheses were based on the conception of particles which, although invisible, were supposed to behave in many ways like visible material ones. Such analogical explanations are not necessarily unscientific. They may be useful or not, depending on whether the choice of model is appropriate.

The modification introduced into the model to make it fit the case is not limited to size. Many fluids, essences, and spirits have been imagined to explain phenomena, and these were obviously conceived on the models of air or smoke or water. But whenever a serious attempt has been made to apply such an explanation consistently, the model has had to be adjusted. If we call the adjusted model *parascheme,* we may use the term *paradigm* for the unadjusted model. Thus we may suppose that the dust motes in a sunbeam served as paradigm for the early atomic hypotheses; then the atoms and their behavior, as conceived in such hypotheses, constitute the parascheme. At first the paradigm may be used with almost no alteration. But if the explanation is of the practical kind, subject to experimental testing, the inadequacy of the model is certain to appear. It is then that adjustments are made.

The history of physics and chemistry affords many illustrations of the use of paraschemes. Fire, heat, and electricity were all at one time regarded as fluid substances. The fact that one body may be heated by another that is hotter, and that the latter loses heat in the process, suggested that what happens in such cases is the transfer of a fluid. The fluid theories of heat were later replaced by a theory of vibrating particles. Vibrations were first realized to be of importance in the explanation of sound, and the relation between pitch and rapidity of vibration was early recognized. Once the vibratory nature of sound had been established and mathematical methods of representing it devised— in the first place in connection with the vibration of strings— a new model was provided for the interpretation and eventual integration (in the theory of the electromagnetic field) of heat, light, and electricity.

H. von Helmholtz (1821-1894) was a German physicist and physiologist who played an important part in introducing this new conception of heat as a form of motion.[42] But he was well aware of the reasonableness and helpfulness of the earlier theory, which posited an imponderable heat substance. Matter without weight may have seemed a contradiction in terms, but every parascheme involves some modification of the paradigm. The atom of the Greek philosopher Democritus (c. 460 - c. 370 B.C.), although essentially a particle of matter, was necessarily deprived of some of the familiar properties of matter, or it would have explained nothing. These properties include weight, bulk, shape, and location; but there are differences between the different states of matter: solids, liquids, and gases. Solids possess all four of the qualities specified, but liquids have no fixed shape (they assume the shape of their container), gases possess neither fixed shape nor fixed bulk (they assume the bulk of their container). Imponderables would also lack weight, and so we may construct a natural scheme of classification as follows:

State	Primary Properties			
	Shape	Bulk	Weight	Place
Solids	X	X	X	X
Liquids	O	X	X	X
Gases	O	O	X	X
Imponderables	O	O	O	X

The fluids that formed the paradigms were the liquids known to ordinary experience. But fluids of all kinds had long before been resolved by some philosophers into solid particles, atoms of minute size. An atomic theory has the merit of explaining not only one kind of phenomenon but a great many. It brings together under one parascheme the different states of matter as well as the different species. To be effective as a parascheme the atom must, as already remarked, be deprived of at least some of the familiar properties of matter. Otherwise one would be explaining a large body simply by alleging that it consisted of a great number of small bodies. Matter is divisible and has a structure, a color, a consistency, a state (solid, liquid, or gaseous), a temperature, and so on, whereas the atoms of Democritus—or at least of the Latin poet Lucretius (who died about 50 B.C.)—were deprived of all properties except shape, size, weight, and motion.[43] Lucretius was concerned to show that all the familiar properties of ordinary matter can be explained as being due to the aggregation of particles that have no other properties except these.[44] It is an important simplification and illustrates the passage from paradigm to parascheme.

Another great advantage of an atomic theory is that it reduces many phenomena that are hard to deal with quantitatively to a form in which the more familiar principles of mechanics and mathematics may be applied. An atom may be supposed to have a velocity, an acceleration, and a spin, to be deflected by collision and to rebound from a surface, or sometimes to penetrate a thin partition; a large number of atoms may be more or less densely packed. Their various aggregations and movements, required for explanatory purposes, may be accounted for by their peculiar shapes. The modern atom is, of course, no longer solid; its shape is described by reference to its constitution and structure. It is, moreover, no longer eternal and indestructible. But it is still without those "secondary" qualities of color, temperature, and consistency by which ordinary matter is known to our senses.

The paraschemes of modern chemistry and physics are mainly of a type that lend themselves to mathematical treatment. For when this is possible the range of deduction is extended, as well as the experimental suggestions. To say that a phenomenon is due to the propagation of waves like the ripples on the surface of still water does not amount to much if such surface ripples are themselves insusceptible of physical measurement and description. But when waves of any kind had been analyzed in terms of amplitude, velocity, frequency, and form (all expressible in mathematical form), the parascheme could be applied and tested in many ways. In later phases of scientific development these mathematical methods grew ever more important, until the equations became the essential part of the parascheme. They constituted, in fact, a very precisely adapted and adaptable mechaneme on which experiments were possible.

The mathematical apparatus has become a general purpose mechaneme, and takes the place of the cruder paraschemes that were the only resource of the earlier philosophers. But the nature of the psychological process has not changed. The new phenomena revealed by observation or experiment, that is, by external peirasis, must be assimilated to some already existing ideas before they can be dealt with in the imagination as material for internal peirasis. If we are to do anything at all about the newly observed process other than by blind experiment, we must first liken it to something that is already known. At first the resources are limited because knowledge is limited; until it has been extended there is but little choice of paradigms by which to explain, judge, and anticipate. But imperfect paradigms serve to guide further experimentation until paraschemes are gradually formed and improved. It is not, of course, only natural phenomena that provide the paradigms.The inventive and technical activities of men result in the production of artificial materials, tools, and machines, and these often provide valuable paradigms for the interpretation of natural phenomena.

Some of the paraschemes I have mentioned depend on the hypothesis of an invisible machinery. If this is merely inaccessible it may eventually become possible by means of an improved technique, as by the use of dissection and the microscope, to discover whether it really exists as supposed. But where the machinery is assumed to be of such a minute structure that it is beyond the reach of any direct examination, the case is rather different. If each hypothetical machinery is to serve a useful purpose it must be related in an intelligible way to the observable phenomena it has to explain. A definite correspondence must be established between the behavior of the machinery and its measurable effects.

The atomic hypotheses are examples of this kind of model, or micromodel, as we may call it. There is no prospect of ever seeing or feeling the individual atoms or studying their behavior directly, but it is supposed (or at least was in the earlier forms of hypothesis) that they behave like objects that are directly observable. Yet what we observe are changes in form, color, bulk, or temperature, and none of these are supposed to occur in the atoms themselves. We have, therefore, to fix certain definite correspondences between the supposed motions of the atoms and the observed changes in the gross matter.

The possibility of establishing such a correspondence is suggested by certain familiar experiences. The well-known change of aspect that objects undergo with increasing distance enables us to conceive the relation between visible aspect and hypothetical micro-behavior. We know, for example, that a swarm of separate objects reduced in size by distance until they are individually invisible may still produce an impression on the sight, although the separate individual objects are now merged into one single continuous object. The movements of the individual objects are no longer visible, but in consequence of them the shape of the single continuous object appears to change. We know that the color of the continuous object need not be the same as that of the individuals. Similiarly we know that a very slow vibration that produces the impression of a succession of separate movements may be speeded up until the movement can no longer be detected; instead of it we seem to observe a distortion of the form of the vibrating object. The obvious connection between sounds and rapid vibrations affords another example of the kind of correspondence that may be relied on in the application of micromodels. The kinetic theory of gases is the classical example of an elaborate correspondence between behavior in a micromodel and observable changes of a quite different nature in the tangible material.

It is in cases of this kind that the question often arises whether such hypothetical machinery exists or not. If no experimental procedure can reveal it, if it is by its nature forever withdrawn from our direct observation, does it serve any legitimate scientific purpose? Since it can only be relied on so far as it is deduced from observable phenomena, what knowledge can it afford us that we have not already gained from these? For a long time the German chemist Wilhelm Ostwald was inclined to deprecate the use of the atomic hypothesis in chemistry (as we have seen, p. 27). Although he admitted that what I have called paraschemes "facilitate further deduction," he implied that their truth can never be demonstrated and that they are therefore to be replaced as soon as possible by the "pure expression of experience," which admits a minimum of uncertainty.[45]

But when one looks for the essential distinction between a para-scheme and this pure expression, it is not easy to find. At first sight it may seem easy to distinguish between a straightforward description of observed facts and a hypothesis that accounts for them by comparing them with some quite distinct set of facts. We must first describe them before we can make the comparison. And yet, at least sometimes, it is only by a comparison that we can give any intelligible description. Mach recognizes this but distinguishes between direct and indirect description. In a chapter of *Die Prinzipien der Wärmelehre* (from which I have already quoted; see p. 105), he points out that for the purpose of communication every new experience must be analyzed as far as possible into generally known elements. This requires comparison. We can only convey our experiences by signs others already understand. Evidently there can exist no sign for an entirely *new* experience, so we must make use of other experiences; to do this we break up the new experience into components that are familiar separately and for which words or signs are available. Thus all description of new ideas must involve some comparison with known ideas.

Mach goes on to say that certain words have come to have a precise meaning in which comparison with concrete objects is no longer discernible. The names of the colors may have originated in a comparison with characteristically colored objects, but the words *red, blue,* and *yellow* have lost all traces of their origin, at least in the mind of the ordinary user. The names of the numbers and of certain simple geometric shapes are of the same kind. Any description that can be made to depend on such words and such words only is, according to Mach, a *direct* description. Thus, if we say of an object that its shape is cubic, its color red, its surface smooth, its consistency tough, and so on, we are confining ourselves to terms that imply no comparison but carry their meaning in themselves. On the other hand, a theory or hypothesis is an indirect description, a description of one phenomenon by comparison with another. The adoption of theories, Mach says, is always dangerous,

> For the theory replaces in our thought a fact A by what is after all a different fact which is simpler or more familiar, and which can represent the former in certain respects in thought, but just because it is not the same can certainly not represent it in some other respect. If now, as may easily happen, enough care is not taken, the most fertile theory can occasionally become an obstacle to investigation. Thus

> the emission theory of light, by accustoming the physicist to regard the trajectory of the light particle as a continuous straight line, can be shown to have made more difficult the recognition of the periodicity of light. . . . On the other hand, if the correspondence between a fact and that which represents it theoretically extends further than the theorizer at first intended, he may be led in this way to unexpected discoveries.[46]

Although Mach was fully aware of the scientific value of hypotheses, which he illustrates abundantly in his books, he regards them only as temporary expedients. They may do useful work and guide the investigator to new ideas and new facts, but they should be discarded as soon as possible.

> In view of these considerations it would seem to be not only advisable but even imperative, while not disdaining the aid of theoretical ideas in research, gradually to replace, as we grow more familiar with the facts, the indirect by the direct description, which no longer contains anything inessential and restricts itself to the abstract presentation of the facts [*die begriffliche Fassung der Tatsachen*].[47]

It would, he says, be impossible to describe every new fact directly, and if the whole range of facts could be presented to us at once we should be bewildered and helpless. Fortunately our attention is at first drawn only to special and unusual things, which we try to make more intelligible by comparing them to everyday things. In this way the common ideas are formed; but as comparisons become more numerous and the subjects of comparison more comprehensive, we gradually arrive at more abstract notions; these permit us to describe things directly. Mach draws a distinction between the "abstract ideas" and the "more or less definite pictorial notions which accompany them" [*den mehr oder weniger bestimmten anschaulichen Vorstellungen, welche die Begriffe begleiten*].

But when we look for examples of these abstract ideas, these direct descriptions that are free from hypothesis, we find only mathematical formulas. He speaks of "a general interpretation of physics free from hypotheses, a physical phenomenology that embraces all domains."[48] Yet what is this physical phenomenology except mathematics? A mathematical mechaneme is devised for dealing with some particular order of events. Later it is found useful for dealing with quite another set of events. In its new use it becomes somewhat modified and adapted to the new facts.

There are now two somewhat different forms of the same mechaneme. Both are available for adaptation to yet further systems of phenomena. By a gradual process of development and differentiation, a multitude of mathematical methods and formulas become available. It is no longer necessary to compare electricity to a fluid, for all those characteristics of a fluid that are shared by electricity can be more precisely expressed mathematically, and the mathematical expression can eliminate all those characteristics that are not shared. Mathematical procedures and formulas thus play the same role as any other paradigm.

It is true that, to the uninitiated, the phenomena to be explained bear no evident relation to the equations. But to the mathematician this relation may be obvious. As with other paradigms the application in experiment leads to modifications and rectifications, and new methods are devised for each particular kind of inquiry. Mathematics has grown into a vast store of tools and methods that in fact constitute a collection of paradigms on which every worker can draw according to his needs. But psychologically the process is the same whether he likens his newly observed set of facts to some other physical and concrete facts as naively conceived or to some system of symbols whose behavior corresponds in the necessary manner to that of the phenomena he is investigating. It is the similarity of behavior that matters.

John Stuart Mill (1806-1873), in his controversy with the British philosopher and historian of science William Whewell (1794-1866), also tried to draw a distinction between hypothesis and description.[49] Mill thought we may explain such a phenomenon as the conduction of heat by saying that it resembles the flow of a fluid in the pores of a conductor, for this is merely a description. But if we say that it *is* a fluid, then we are committing ourselves to a statement that must be either true or false. In the former case it can only be a question of whether the description is accurate, and many descriptions based on comparison with different phenomena might be equally accurate. Thus we might say that the conduction of heat also resembled the transmission of vibrations, and this description would not be incompatible with the other. But we should not be justified in saying that heat actually consists in vibrations and is at the same time a fluid. Either it is a fluid or it is not. But it might *resemble* a fluid more or less.

This seems to be the distinction made by Mill. It can be accepted only if we suppose that men making such comparisons actually suppose that their chosen paradigm is perfect. Yet, as we have seen, even the ancient atomists did not suppose their ultimate particles to be actual portions of matter; they endowed them with special qualities. Descartes did not suppose his vortices to be exactly like vortices in a material fluid;[50] he had to make certain arbitrary assumptions about the ether in which they occurred. The believers in caloric did not regard it as ordinary matter, for they deprived it of weight. The electric fluid was never conceived to be exactly like water, or even like heat, for in that case nothing would have been explained. Such comparisons inevitably involve some modification of the paradigm. Probably no ancient astronomer ever supposed that the planets were carried around on material wheels. If they used such words, it was because no other words were available. Nowadays we employ geometric or even algebraic expressions, and do not realize that we are making any comparison at all.

13 *The Nature of Play*

The tendency to play, common among the higher vertebrates, poses the following questions: What distinguishes play from work? What is its biological function? From what more general function did it originate? In the case of human beings, how does the urge to play enter into other activities? The importance of play in relation to the psychology of art has been generally recognized, but its relation to science is often overlooked.

I shall start by considering some theories (from the end of the 19th century or the beginning of the 20th) on the nature and function of play. Herbert Spencer was, perhaps, the first to approach the question from the biological point of view.[51] He regarded play as the spontaneous activity of an animal, which, while overflowing with energy, has no necessary business to perform. Under pressure of need an animal's behavior is adapted to that need; but when there is no such pressure it still feels the urge for action and then its behavior takes the form of play. The lower animals, Spencer says, are unceasingly occupied in searching for food, escaping from enemies, forming places of shelter, and making preparations for progeny. But the superior efficiency of the higher animals enables appetites to be satisfied more easily, leaving a surplus of vigor; in addition, the greater variety of faculty in these animals produces the same result. All the faculties cannot be employed together, and in those that remain unexercised for a considerable time the unused energy accumulates and issues in the form of play. He also argues that the satisfaction an animal feels in fulfilling the promptings of its instincts is partially experienced when similar behavior occurs merely as play. Dogs in their mimic chasing and fighting, kittens running after a cotton ball derive "an ideal satisfaction for the destructive instincts in the absence of real satisfaction for them."

When he speaks of human games, Spencer stresses still more the partial satisfaction of the basic instincts. He does not mean their biological satisfaction (which would be inconsistent with his whole theory) but rather pleasure or enjoyment, a psychological satisfaction of the feelings, which although it corresponds to no realization of any biological end provides a stimulus for the continuance of the same activity. Boys chasing one another, wrestling, and making prisoners "obviously gratify in a partial way the predatory instincts." Even in games of skill, practiced by children or adults, "the satisfaction is in achieving victory—in getting the better of an antagonist." The love of conquest can obtain gratification from a victory at chess in the absence of ruder victories. There are two sources of satisfaction: that connected with the instinctive action which the play mimics, and that associated with the activity itself.

> This activity of the intellectual faculties in which they are not used for purposes of guidance in the business of life, is carried on partly for the sake of the pleasure of the activity itself, and partly for the accompanying satisfaction of certain egoistic feelings which find for the moment no other sphere.[52]

Neither of these satisfactions is to be confounded with the "ulterior benefit" to the animal or to the species, which is the normal consequence of all business activities. It is the entire absence of this ulterior benefit which, for Spencer, distinguishes play. He even speaks as if the other satisfactions were the same in both play and business. Yet it can hardly be said that the satisfaction a dog derives from vanquishing a rival in battle is the same as it gets from indulging in a friendly tussle; nor that the joy in victory, when it occurs in sport, is the same as that which follows victory in a life-and-death struggle. When a bitch plays with her puppies, no observer could suppose that any considerable part of the "satisfaction" that all seem to derive from the game was due to consciousness of victory or success or any similar "egoistic feeling." If human games, especially those of older children and adults, do contain an important element of this kind, it is something that arises from another source and is not an essential part of the play.

The next major writer on play is the German philosopher Karl Groos (1861-1946) who maintains that it has the function of preparing the young animal for the future business of life, and has been specially evolved for this purpose. He says:

> The play of young animals has its origin in the fact that certain very important instincts appear at a time when the animal does not seriously need them. . . . Its utility consists in the practice and exercise it affords for some of the more important duties of life, inasmuch as selection tends to weaken the blind force of instinct, and aids more and more the development of independent intelligence as a substitute for it. At the moment when intelligence is sufficiently evolved to be more useful in the struggle for existence than the most perfect instinct, then will selection favour those individuals in whom the instincts appear earlier and in less elaborated forms—in forms that . . . are merely for . . . practice and exercise—that is to say that it

> will favour those animals which play. . . . Animals cannot be said to play because they are young and frolicsome, but rather they have a period of youth in order to play; for only by so doing can they supplement the insufficient hereditary endowment with individual experience, in view of the coming tasks of life.[53]

Interpreting this according to the theory of instinct I outlined in Chapter 7, we may say that play is associated with the generalized instincts and provides the raw material, so to speak, for trial-and-error behavior. Groos points to play which is a form of experimentation and consists in random efforts without immediate aim, but yields knowledge of the properties of the external world. It constitutes a kind of rudimentary physics or experimental mechanics adapted to the needs of the animal. Trial-and-error behavior must frequently lead to new combinations, both between the animal's own actions and between his actions and the changing elements of the situation. In this way, through the formation of new habits, his behavior is gradually better adapted to the environment. In behavior of this kind, which Groos calls "intelligent" as distinct from instinctive, actions are necessarily more or less vague and undirected until habits have been formed. The capacity for forming new habits implies this. But it is still a question how such behavior could ever have arisen if in more primitive animals all behavior was of the stereotyped kind.

Groos does not confine himself to the biological explanation but tackles the psychological aspect of the problem when he attributes the play tendency to pleasure in the possession of power, to "delight in the control we have over our bodies and over external objects." He adds:

> The young bear that plays in the water, the dog that tears a paper into scraps, the ape that delights in producing new and uncouth sounds, the sparrow that exercises its voice, the parrot that smashes its feeding trough—all experience the pleasure in energetic activity, which is, at the same time, joy in being able to accomplish something.[54]

Groos makes a broad distinction between mere experimental manipulations and more specialized forms of play such as mimic hunting or fighting. But according to Lloyd Morgan, both have the same essential function.[55] The former is concerned with the progressive coordination of simple movements that form the components of *all* behavior, whereas the latter are related to the more specialized and elaborate activities that are broadly determined by heredity but are subject to improvements and refinements through practice and experience. With regard to the more elaborate forms of play, Lloyd Morgan does not accept Groos's view that in some animals instincts are prematurely developed. He sees the great difference, both biological and psychological, between the friendly tussle and the real combat. He is inclined to regard the play activity as a specially evolved instinct, one that has

> . . . evolved directly as a preparation, as a means of experimentation through which certain essential modes of skill were acquired—those animals in which the preparatory play propensity was not inherited in due force and requisite amount being worsted in the combats of later life, and eliminated in the struggle for existence. For, in the preparatory tussles and squabbles and playful fights of young animals, experience is gained without serious risk to life and limb.[56]

This may be true, but it leaves us asking how such a novel instinct could have arisen, and it also fails to explain why play activity should continue throughout life in many animals as well as in man.

In sum, for the biologist it is not quite enough to explain that a particular form of behavior is useful. He will still ask how it could have arisen in the first place. From what earlier or more general form of behavior could it have been adapted or specialized? In explaining the origin of any organ the biologist always looks for some earlier structure that might, under imaginable circumstances, have been modified so as to give rise to it. So, in explaining behavior, we must look for a more generalized type, common to a wider class of animals, from which the type in question could have been derived. When we have found such a generalized form of behavior and recognized it as the precursor of the specialized form, we can sometimes see that from the same generalized precursor other specialized forms may also have been developed, though in a different direction, and that there have thus arisen a number of distinct types, no longer obviously connected with another yet in fact related through a common ancestry. This, I think, is the case in the present instance.

It is obvious enough that animals in the course of their play may contract habits that are of no value to them at all, and may even be harmful. It is not only useful reactions that are established after experimental behavior. When a definite state of tension is released as a result of some action performed during trial-and-error behavior, that action tends to be established. But when no special state of tension is involved—as we are assuming in the case of play—then, if habits are nevertheless established, it must be for some other reason. If in the course of play some particular combination of movements is selected for repetition and becomes habitual, we must then look for some new principle of selection. If there is no strong desire present at the time, the result cannot be attributed to the satisfaction of the desire.

Thorndike's experiments can help at this point. We recall that he placed cats and dogs in cages from which they were able to escape only if they pressed a lever, pulled a string, and so on (see above, p. 15). The time taken to learn the way out in a series of trials was graphed, and Thorndike summed up his results in two "laws," one of which he calls "the law of exercise," namely:

> Any response to a situation will, other things being equal, be more strongly connected with the situation in proportion to the number of times it has been connected with that situation and to the average vigor and duration of the connections.[57]

In other words, simple repetition makes for the establishment of linkage. Pavlov's experiments also show that repetition is a factor that is always effective though not always indispensable. Thus we may expect that any circumstances that lead to the frequent performance of an action sequence will result in the formation of a habit, even if no definite state of tension is involved. But there can be no action at all without some inward prompting, and although such prompting may be general and undirected, it may be supposed to have the same fundamental nervous basis as the more organized states of tension that are able to restrict behavior within certain limits and direct it toward a goal.

The Scottish psychologist and physiologist Alexander Bain (1818-1903) maintained that unless we admit the normal occurrence of spontaneous behavior, we cannot give an explanation of any kind of experimental behavior.[58] He showed that the development of the "will," of voluntary behavior, can only be accounted for if we suppose it to be based on a preceding spontaneous behavior. His argument applies only to "conscious" control, and this he understands when he speaks of the "will." He declared that there can be no will to act in a certain way unless the action has already been experienced. The argument is put even more forcefully by the American psychologist William James (1842-1910) as follows:

> If in voluntary action, properly so-called, the act must be foreseen, it follows that no creature not endowed with divinatory power can perform an act voluntarily for the first time. . . . As we must wait for . . . sensations to be given us, so we must wait for . . . movements to be performed involuntarily before we can frame ideas of what either of these things are. . . . When a particular movement, having once occurred in a random, reflex, or involuntary way, has left an image of itself in the memory, then the movement can be desired again, proposed as an end, and deliberately willed.[59]

It is not, of course, suggested that the "spontaneous" action is without cause. Bain discussed at length the circumstances that "govern" the spontaneous discharge, even though he knew nothing of the influence of hormones on the nervous system. And he did not deny that all kinds of reflex actions occur for the first time in response to specific stimuli. He was concerned with learned behavior, and although he did not express the matter in terms that are familiar today, he was really maintaining that an animal cannot learn to associate a particular action with a particular situation unless that action is able to occur independently. Further, if learning implies the linking together of various actions not previously connected, by the progressive selection and arrangement of components first produced at random, then we must assume a tendency to produce these random acts before we can begin to explain the process of selection. Moreover, if these random acts from which the selection has to be made are already linked inseparably with particular stimuli, then the learned complex reaction will never be repeatable unless those particular stimuli are also repeated. The components of behavior that are to be compounded in a new habit must be sufficiently independent to begin with.

Thus we must suppose that animals—at least those animals which have any capacity for learning—must have at their disposal, as it were, a fund of unattached activity from which they can draw the materials for their new acquirements. Such activity may require some general stimulus, but this is as likely to be of internal as of external origin. As Bain says:

> Youth and health, the plentiful nourishment and absence of drain, the damming up of the accumulating charge by temporary restraint—are predisposing causes of a great and sudden outburst, during which the individual's capability is at the highest pitch.[60]

A state of excitement may be brought about by various causes, which he mentions; however:

> Whatever may be the cause . . . one effect arising from it is an increase in the vehemence of all the spontaneous impulses occurring at the moment.[61]

This state of excitement may be regarded as a state of tension that prompts to activity but not to activity of any special kind. Unlike some other states of tension, it is not brought into existence by some particular external situation or any particular state of physiological disequilibrium. It arises when the body is in its most normal and healthy condition, when all the essential needs of the animal have been satisfied, when it is under no pressure to act in any particular manner or for any particular goal. It may be due to hormonal activity, to the nervous tonus, to all kinds of internal stimulations that occur in a healthy and vigorous animal, but it seems to evoke activity without bias—sheer activity.

It is evident that this view of spontaneous activity is closely connected with Spencer's account of play. It is also clear that the relation of such spontaneous activity to learning and the formation of habits is what Groos and Morgan have in mind when they say that play is an exercise and training for life. It is not hard to see that organized play—that is to say, traditional games and sport—may have arisen from unorganized play in just the same way that other complex forms of behavior originated from experimental behavior. All intelligent behavior, or all learned behavior, can have no other origin. If this generalized activity without specific goal is to be called play, then it is certainly not a prerogative of youth and childhood; it is the raw material of all learned behavior. If it occurs more rarely in the adult than in the adolescent, this is because so much of the behavior of the former has already been organized and reduced to regular habits. If it occurs more rarely in other animals than in man, it is because under natural conditions most animals have to work too hard for their living to find leisure for undirected activities. In domesticated animals that have such leisure, play occupies a much larger portion of their existence; and in mammals generally, whose young remain for a time under the protection of their parents, there is opportunity for play during the early months of life.

We must distinguish, therefore, between play in this general sense—mere undirected activity, activity for its own sake—and the organized play that becomes so prominent in human society. The latter is a special development, which may be compared with art, dancing, ritual, and any other organized and traditional form of activity that does not appear to serve any obvious biological end. It has ceased to be undirected activity.

It is governed by rigid traditions and kept alive by new emotions and purposes and comes in many cases to acquire a direct relation with fundamental biological needs. Thousands of people in modern society earn their livelihood by playing games, dancing, singing, practicing the arts and performing rituals, and their attitude to these activities cannot be distinguished psychologically from that of the millions who plough the fields or tend their flocks or engage in the immemorial arts and crafts.

But we are not concerned with these developments here. I wish rather to draw attention to the part played by undirected behavior—the overflow of activity, the doing of things for the sake of doing rather than for the sake of the thing done—in invention and scientific inquiry. This merely means that the play which serves in childhood to provide the experimental activity from which useful forms of behavior may be acquired continues to serve throughout life, for those who enjoy the leisure for it, in much the same way. The experimental activities of adults may be directed toward definite ends, in which case they are likely to be restricted and guided in narrow channels. But often they are carried on without any such direction and for their own sake. The adult scientist working in his laboratory experiences the same kind of pleasure in his activity that the child does playing with blocks in the nursery. If this urge to play were not present, then what is called "pure science" would excite no interest. It is true that the scientist, when challenged, may assert that his work is not without some practical purpose and value, even if it is only that one can never be sure that something of practical value will not emerge if one perseveres with any line of investigation. But it is hardly credible that such vague possibilities should form the main incentive to abstract inquiries concerning the origin of the remoter galaxies, the magnetic field of the moon, the fauna and flora of the polar regions, or the geographical distribution of the water wagtail. Those who pursue such inquiries are sometimes eager to disclaim any concern for practical applications.

In order to explain this kind of irrational activity some psychologists have imagined an instinct of curiosity. However, as William James says, what might be regarded as such an instinct in animals has but little connection with what we call scientific curiosity.[62] The Scottish philosopher David Hume (1711-1776) discusses the "love of truth" and recognizes that no man can love the truth for its own sake. Any number of trivial truths may be discovered by anybody with scarcely an effort, and yet few people avail themselves of this possibility. Something else is required to make truth attractive, namely,

> . . . the genius and capacity which is employed in its invention and discovery. What is easy and obvious is never valued; and even what is *in itself* difficult, if we come to the knowledge of it without difficulty, and without any stretch of thought or judgment, is but little regarded.[63]

He mentions other necessary conditions that need not be considered for the moment. We are not concerned primarily with the quest for truth but rather with any kind of experimental activity and the pleasure that is to be had from it. For the tendency a man shows to engage in a particular form of activity may conveniently be equated with the pleasure he derives from it. This pleasure may in the end be nothing but the relief from the intolerable discomfort of not yielding to a habit, as in the case of an addict. It may be that all forms of pleasure have something of this negative character.

This view—that what makes truth, or the search for truth, attractive is the "genius and capacity" employed in its discovery—is perhaps not very different from Groos's view that the pleasure of play is in achievement. Though all normal activity is pleasurable to a healthy animal, if the activity is too restricted or too simple its continued repetition will quickly induce fatigue, or, in the case of a mental activity, tedium. On the other hand if it is an activity involving the whole or the greater part of the body, or many parts in succession, the distribution and alternation of effort will allow the maximum expenditure of energy with the minimum of local fatigue. Where the activity is mental, we may suppose that the greater the number of ideas and the greater the variety of mental sequences, the less readily will the pleasurable exertion be neutralized by boredom.

In either case, bodily or mental, the activity must not produce strain, and it must not require exertions beyond the strength and ability of the animal. Thus people find most pleasure in exercising their best powers, in working near the limit of their intellectual capacity rather than in doing what is too easy. The same principle holds for physical activities and for all kinds of bodily skills. The greatest satisfaction is to be had from work that calls for the highest skill a person possesses and not from the endless performance of simple tasks. Of course, in human society men and women have the additional satisfaction of finding their achievements applauded, but it is obvious that the pleasure may be very great without this; even animals, who cannot be suspected of vanity, seem to prefer to practice their more elaborate performances.

This preference for more complex kinds of activity explains why the play of animals so often seems to assume the chief forms of adult behavior. For in general it is these performances that represent the best that is in the power of the animal—that is to say, the forms of behavior that make the highest normal demands on the animal's capacity. The very young can only make unorganized movements with their limbs; their nervous organization does not yet provide for the complicated sequences of fighting, running, climbing. But as they develop and as new powers are attained, each new accomplishment becomes the favorite form of play. Man is conscious of his skill and can measure his attainments by comparison with those of his companions, and this alters the psychological character of his play. But it cannot be maintained that there is not a pleasurable sense of achievement which is independent of all rivalry, and which is proportionate to the nervous complexity of the behavior.

The tendency of play to assume more complex forms is also of biological significance. For if play is an essential means for the further elaboration of intelligent behavior, it is most likely to be fruitful if it operates near the limits of what has already been achieved, whence new advances must be made. If adult human play is to be fruitful in invention and discovery, it too must operate near the boundaries of existing knowledge. Although individuals of limited capacity may get as much satisfaction from a simple operation as the more gifted may get from one far more complex, yet if everyone devotes play activities to those operations that he finds the more exacting, a general tendency toward the acquisition of new skills and new knowledge will be the result.

Play, then, is in the beginning merely the spontaneous activity natural to every healthy and vigorous animal. Insofar as an animal is already adapted to certain situations, its behavior in relation to them is more or less regular and stereotyped. But in many animals such adaptation is imperfect during adolescence and has to be improved by experience. Such animals are no less active than the others, but their actions are not at first related in a definite way to their situations. Their behavior appears random and inappropriate. But such is the nature of these animals that, in general, those of their actions which happen to be useful are encouraged and those which are not useful or harmless are discouraged; thus, little by little, out of the repertoire of random performances useful forms of behavior are selected and organized. Behavior begins to appear less random, more purposeful, and more adapted to the animal's obvious needs. In the intervals between passages of purposeful behavior bouts of the old unorganized activity still occur. It is these that are usually called play.

In the course of time, as the animal grows older and behavior becomes organized into various types of useful activity, these types gradually invade the periods of play. That is to say, the interludes of random activity become less random and assume certain regular forms; these forms are outwardly similar to those that belong to the animal's organized behavior. But the resemblance is only outward for, although these organized forms of play simulate business and purposeful activities, they do not serve any corresponding purpose, and in various ways they differ radically from business activities and are adapted gradually for a different function. In young animals this kind of play serves to exercise and train the faculties and provides raw material for the formation of new habits. In the adult it provides an opportunity for discovery and invention. Accidental discoveries have been important in the history of inventions and are more likely to be noted in play than in work. If a man is concentrating on a particular purpose, he will, it is true, note at once any accidental circumstance that seems to help him or suggest a method of accomplishing his aim. But anything with no connection to his immediate preoccupation—however important and interesting it is in some other connection—is likely to be overlooked. On the other hand, when there is no particular purpose or preoccupation, any slightly unusual sequence may catch his attention and lead to repetition and perhaps discovery. Thus play, just because it *is* carried on for no particular purpose, may in many cases be more fruitful in new ideas than deliberate investigation and eager search.[64]

14 *Cultural Differentiation and the Origin of Poetry*

In man the process of cultural differentiation leads to ever new forms of activity as the primitive forms are progressively affected by new and changing conditions. Differentiation is a fundamental biological process, and all evolutionary processes in plants and animals lead to it. When many similar organisms are subjected to different conditions, they undergo different changes, so that as a result a variety of new organisms arises from the single original type. The same process occurs in the development of the elements of culture. The simple tool, improved and developed under different conditions and for different purposes, becomes the ancestor of a whole family of distinct implements. And if we compare the ancestor with its progeny, we find in the former some rudiments of all the special features of its descendants. In the case of behavior, the process is necessarily different. The original types of behavior vary within fairly wide limits, and particular variants become increasingly stereotyped in relation to particular functions. Generalized biological types are those from which we can suppose a number of distinct specialized types to have been derived. Generalized cultural features may, in the same way, be regarded as those from which, by a process of differentiation, later features have been developed.

Play is the ancestor of many specialized descendants. From the primitive play tendency—the restless urge to employ one's faculties and exert one's powers, which occupies every moment not claimed by urgent business or by sleep—there have developed certain special types of behavior that have in common the fact that they serve no biological end. They serve, however, a special function inasmuch as they encourage friendly cooperation or channel dangerous rivalry and antisocial tendencies into less harmful forms of behavior. Such special types of behavior, which grow more elaborate as they are further differentiated, include much of what is usually classed as religion, art, and sport, as well as much of science. These developments cannot, of course, be explained in terms of the play tendency alone, since we have to seek the special conditions that guided the differentiation. But the whole process must remain unintelligible unless we can find its starting point.

I have written elsewhere about the process of differentiation from primitive efforts at communication, which lead finally to the conventional human languages of today.[65] I have there argued that before any adequate language of sounds was invented, there existed a language of signs, resting fundamentally on the principle of pantomime; and that it is impossible to account for the development of human communication unless we assume that all kinds of *conventional* language must have been preceded by a *natural* or *self-explanatory* language. Oral language is almost exclusively conventional; the element of onomatopoeia is negligible. In the beginning, when communication was still tentative, convention must have been entirely absent, and only those signs that conveyed their meaning directly would have been useful. In the first stages of communication the idea to be conveyed was expressed by all sorts of activities—by dramatic gestures (for example, jumping high to suggest the idea 'tall') or by plastic representation (drawings or models of a thing or a tool to suggest the idea of that thing). All these activities were, however, related by the common primary purpose, namely that of inducing another man to perform some desired action and of generating in his mind the idea of the action to be performed. But these activities had other effects besides those aimed at, and each mode of communicating turned out to be adapted to some subsidiary use. In the end, the original function of communication has come to be performed almost exclusively by conventionalized sounds, and the other forms have been adapted for quite different purposes. Thus dramatic gestures, besides their extensive development in relation to religious ritual and magic, have found their place in one of the more important forms of art. From the plastic forms of language have grown the art of sculpture and the scientific technique of constructing models. Graphic gestures, the representation of things by plans or drawings in two dimensions, have developed into the art of painting.

Conventionalized oral language is the ancestral form from which poetry has arisen by means of differentiation. The emergence of poetry from the techniques of communication illustrates the way in which serious occupations give rise to forms of play.[66]

Many have attributed poetry to some kind of artistic instinct in man, but this seems gratuitous. The biologist would ask why such an instinct should have arisen. We can understand that the conspicuous instincts in animals arose from the need for food, the need for self-defense, the need to continue the race, and—in social animals—the need to keep the group from disintegrating. But how could one explain an artistic instinct?

We may admit not an artistic instinct but a natural tendency in early man to produce patterned sound (like the baby's *da, da*). Such sound seems to give pleasure to the maker, and this provides a basis for his persistence in the activity. From such beginnings there could result such sophistications as "hey diddle diddle, the cat and the fiddle." But it is not easy to see how this could have led in due course to the use of assonance, rhyme, alliteration, imagery (and other features of what has traditionally been regarded as poetry) in discourse that has an intelligible content. In other words, making rhythmic noises for pleasure is one thing; using rhythmic features for the purpose of communication is another. Why has man not been content to communicate in prose?

It can be plausibly argued that some of the characteristic features of what has been regarded as poetry through the centuries owe their prevalence to their mnemonic value. Before writing existed in any form that permitted the recording of actual words—and by this I exclude any kind of picture writing or conventional hieroglyphs that record ideas and facts but not their linguistic expression—there was need for much memorizing. Magical sayings, long rubrics attached to religious rituals, narratives of past events, royal proclamations, oracular utterances—all such had to be committed to memory by somebody if they were to be preserved and handed on to the next generation. It would be only too easy for the form of words to vary as memories failed, and alternative versions would come to exist side by side to demonstrate the failure. Any means of aiding the memory and preventing such variation that presented itself would tend to be encouraged and adopted.

Sentences with a special rhythm, marked alliteration, or rhyme not only would stay in the memory more readily but also would more easily betray any alteration that did creep in. Repetitions are also easily memorized. Repetition may happen unintentionally where only short word sequences are concerned. But when longer sequences are already learned by heart, they are available as convenient formulas whenever required.[67]

All this may seem rather speculative. But nothing can now remain of the earliest compositions. Until the invention of some kind of phonetic writing they could not be recorded except by tradition, and we cannot expect them to have survived thousands of years of war and migration. The material on which our theories of the origin of poetry must be based consists of the written records of the oldest civilizations and the observations of explorers among primitive peoples. From these we have to try and reconstruct the beginnings. And we must try to explain the later developments evidenced in the poetry of civilized peoples.

It is not necessary to suppose that devices such as repetition were deliberately invented in the first place for the purpose of aiding the memory. But sentences and passages marked by such mnemonic virtues arising by chance would be more easily retained; and in due course their value would be appreciated. Many early inventions may well have begun with chance discoveries. Once the advantages of such forms were recognized they would be adopted deliberately. The devices employed would vary with each particular language: in some a rhythm of stress, in others of quantity, in yet others alliteration or rhyme. Sometimes a regularity of form based on regular repetition would be developed.

All these methods can be illustrated from the extant poetry of different peoples. It is well known that the verse of the ancient Hebrews lacks both meter and rhyme but displays "a rhythm produced by parallel clauses, generally in sets of two." These clauses are "expected to be approximately equal in length, but it is equally important for them to be cognate in meaning and parallel in grammatical structure."[68] An example is Job 22:9-10:

> Thou hast sent widows away empty,
> And the arms of the fatherless have been broken.
> Therefore snares are round about thee
> And sudden fear troubleth thee.

Chinese poetry also lacks meter but relies on rhyme to mark the end of each line, and provide the ear with a resting-place.[69] Greek and Latin could do without rhyme because they had such clear meters. English poetry can also do without it where the meter is uniform and clear (as in iambic verse), and blank verse has come to mean five-foot iambs. In French poetry metrical rhythm has practically disappeared, but rhyme is important. Thus the poetic conventions of different languages all achieve, by quite independent means, the same end of dividing discourse into clear units.

Patterned language, whether or not it began merely because it gave pleasure, was in time seen to be useful for a practical operation, that of recording in words important information (and also magical verbal rituals) in a way that causes the least burden on the memory and the least risk of distortion. As in other crafts, in proportion as the skill required increases, the satisfaction in achievement increases too. The work of the poet was highly skilled, and, as elsewhere, practice in the skill led to decorative extensions. Beyond the degree of rhythm or verbal echoing that was needed for the easy retention of the passage, there was developed a minute code of rules, to be followed for their own sake, for the mere exercise of more skill.

Many of the oldest extant compositions are poems, and the reason for this is obvious enough; the more important matters had to be put into metrical form—if they were to be remembered at all—before writing was available. This meant that, by the time writing had been invented, metrical form had become associated with important and solemn matters, and so continued to be used to record them. It was naturally the records of the important matters that were carefully preserved and have come down to us. Elements of regularity, occurring either by chance or introduced because they were found pleasurable, were preserved and copied because of their utility for those who had to recite compositions relating to important religious or social matters. The value of rhythm, rhyme, assonance, alliteration, repetition of phrases, the constant association of epithets, and other devices would be discovered gradually, through experience in memorizing long passages.

In time there would come to exist a recognizable difference between the language of important statements (religious, royal, traditional) that had to be preserved, and the common language of daily intercourse. While the spoken language changed—rapidly in communities where it was unprotected by writing—the language of these ancient compositions remained fixed, and so came to be characterized by archaisms, which were not always clearly understood, and sometimes by unintelligible expressions. These could only have been eliminated from old poetry by translating it and substituting modern words. But the maintenance of the metrical form would make this almost impossible, and where the text was sacred, no alteration of any kind could be permitted. In religious and magic rituals the archaic has a special sanctity. Men who observe practices they do not understand must be careful to observe them faithfully for fear of omitting something essential. If the harvest fails, if the ghosts of the departed return, if the hunting is bad or the tribe defeated in battle, nobody can point to the exact element in the preparatory rites whose omission or improper observance was responsible for what went wrong. Here one can only rely on tradition and alter as little as possible. Thus in all matters of this kind, when much is at stake and nobody knows very clearly how effects are in fact produced, there is a special need to preserve the ancient rites in all their details (see p. 142). Thus we find old languages, old forms of dress, old methods of killing, old methods of making fire, and so on as constituent elements in such rituals.

For all these reasons, an archaic form of language came to be associated with poetry, which preserved past traditions in old words fixed by the poetic devices. Gilbert Murray says that the poetry of Homer and

Hesiod is "demonstrably traditional," "full of ancient and obscure words, some of which are used wrongly in the actual poems."[70] Archaisms became associated with the solemn matters treated in poetry; this association made them seem solemn and impressive, which in turn led poets to use them deliberately, even to invent their own. W. G. Aston, writing on Japanese poetry, notes that it includes words that are "survivals from a very archaic stage of the language," and that "the meaning of some of them is now extremely doubtful, a circumstance which forms no obstacle whatever to their continued use."[71]

Since poets are not always philologists, their archaisms are sometimes rather artificial. Shelley uses *glode* as the past tense of *glide.* Swinburne uses the forms *I weet* and *wote.* Sometimes the poet is glad to invent such forms because they provide a rhyme or are more easily fitted into his meter. It is, for instance, convenient to have the word *inly* to replace the usual *inwardly,* provided, of course, that one is not barred from using the ordinary word as well where it fits better. It is convenient to be able to invent a dissyllable *paven* for the usual monosyllable *paved.* These examples from Swinburne could easily be supplemented. And why should the poet not use such forms? If queer words taken from a former age are effective to a reader who knows nothing of their origin, why should not the poet invent a few strange forms for himself? This seems to be what Aristotle implies in a famous passage in which he says that the virtue of poetic diction

> . . . is to be clear and not mean. The clearest is that made up of the ordinary words for things, but it is mean . . . To be impressive and avoid commonness, diction must use unfamiliar terms, by which I mean strange words, metaphors, lengthened forms, and everything out of the ordinary. (*Poetics,* paragraph 22)

The "lengthened forms" are in fact archaisms, or fanciful forms resembling archaisms. When an Attic poet used the old, uncontracted form of some word that was traditional in epic, he seemed to Aristotle—and no doubt to himself—to be lengthening the normal form. Gilbert Murray mentions, as a modern parallel, the use of obsolete verbal terminations like *thou goest, he goeth.*[72]

When later poets and philosophers began to reflect on this matter of style, they were as unable as Aristotle had been to give reasons for the rules they proposed. The ideas about poetry that resulted are somewhat like those which were invoked to explain early magical practices that had survived. As man does not understand the origin of his religious ideas, so he understands nothing of the origin of his ideas of art. But this strengthens rather than weakens his sentiments about them. He commonly resents any suggestion that they may be explained anthropologically, psychologically, or historically. He prefers to interpret them mystically. The critics knew from their own experience that they were affected by certain forms but did not know why. They felt that elevated diction was essential to poetry but could give no reason for this. Yet the belief that it was so led poets to indulge deliberately in all kinds of quaint affectations. In England we have the metaphysical poets in the sixteenth and seventeenth centuries; in France, the *précieux* and *précieuses* in the seventeenth; in Spain the followers of Góngora at about the same time; and in Italy, the fashion set by Marini. There have probably always been some to protest against affectation, cleverness, pretended profundity, and meaningless verbiage. But the very existence of poetry implies the use of a special language, and the elimination of all forms of *préciosité* would put an end to all versification. For practical purposes prose expression is always used now. Poetry is still pleasing for its own sake, especially to those who have been trained to appreciate it; but where the substance is more important than the form, where something of interest and significance has to be imparted, the best and clearest language cannot brook the arbitrary and severe restraints imposed by verse.

The origin of another poetic device, namely rhythm, is doubtless not entirely mnemonic but due in part to the early association of speech with the dance. All animal movements that have to be repeated tend to acquire a rhythm, since there is an ideal interval between the successive acts. We see this not only in the fundamental physiological processes but in nearly all forms of locomotion (at least in the higher animals), in scratching, licking, chewing, and in human operations with tools, such as sawing, chopping, hammering, polishing, and so forth. Dancing in its most unsophisticated form is a generalized exertion of the whole mobile apparatus, and since the continuation of such movement involves repetition, a rhythm inevitably develops. Accompanying vocal utterances would naturally come to assume the rhythm of the bodily movement, even if they had not been designed for this purpose. And if the words did not fit it, they would in time be modified until they did. Later still, these rhythmical word sequences were recited without external musical accompaniment: poetry was emancipated from music and the dance. Then, since the absence of a rhythmic accompaniment excluded the possibility of a conflict of rhythms, the rhythm of the verse became less regular and less rigid. But the poet nevertheless contrived to make the metrical stresses fall on words or syllables that are naturally stressed. To achieve this, he would often find it necessary to introduce an unnatural word order, and in time, this peculiarity came to be associated with poetry. It was then copied and done deliberately where it was unnecessary, because it was felt to be part of the poetic style.

Religious ceremonial activities develop (or degenerate) into a mode of recreation. The dance, the song, the dramatic performance, the long recitation of heroic exploits and of the activities of the gods—all, perhaps, religious in origin—were preserved and developed because of the direct enjoyment they afforded. This enjoyment often consisted in a kind of intoxication, and genuine intoxication by drugs often formed part of the celebration. The dancer or singer worked himself into a frenzy, and the effect was contagious. All such emotional effects became linked by association with the language used on such occasions.

Rhythm, alliteration, sound harmonies, and so on are today capable, in themselves, of producing emotional effects, and these are not accounted for by a mnemonic origin. We may perhaps agree that rhythm in dance and song, from which lyric poetry came, was probably always emotionally effective, and that once poetry was emancipated from the dance, its rhythm may have continued to produce emotional effects directly. We may also agree that poetic characters that cannot be traced to the dance, such as rhyme or alliteration, originated because they were directly pleasurable. Nevertheless, it seems likely that the later use of these features as mnemonics in poetry of great religious or social importance meant that in time their emotional effects were greatly enhanced. For the long association of such poetic characteristics with verbal sequences that were uttered only in strongly emotional circumstances ensured that the emotion should come in the end to be linked to the forms themselves. The very nature of the original poetic compositions was such as to make them of emotional significance, since they were not concerned with trivialities but were recited on special solemn occasions. Again, it is because these solemn utterances were frequently archaic in form that the archaic form eventually acquired the power of exciting emotion; finally archaic language was deliberately chosen by poets in order to have such an emotional effect.

Thus, to explain some of the emotional effect of certain forms of words I am appealing to association. A familiar example is the language of the *Book of Common Prayer,* which in English-speaking countries has come to be associated with the solemnities of the burial service and other liturgies. Serious communications expressed in this language acquire a certain dignity from the association. The emotions that prevail in the presence of situations in which this language is normal are to some extent excited by it even in other situations. If there is too great a contrast between the nature of the situation and the language, then revulsion or laughter may result, according to circumstances. But for the present I am merely concerned to call attention to the transfer of emotional effect from the solemn ritual to another situation through the medium of language.

The suggestion that the poetic characteristics of language became prevalent for unpoetic reasons but were retained because they were found to be aesthetically effective is—if it is true—merely another instance of something that has often happened in the history of literature: namely, a certain form originated or was developed for reasons that had nothing to do with aesthetic effect, but was retained because in time it came to have such an effect. Perhaps the best-known example is the chorus in Greek tragedy. Greek tragedy probably evolved from a choral dance in honor of a deity, and the chorus, in the earliest plays, presumably was a survival from this primitive religious rite. But why was the chorus retained by later tragedians? A. W. Schlegel suggested that it was because it was found to be useful aesthetically for the purpose of commenting on the action of the play. When the actors leave the stage the chorus sings odes that comment on the situation in a manner impossible (without implausibility) for the actors directly involved in it. Schlegel calls the chorus the personified reflection on the action of the play, the poet's own sympathetic view, as representative and spokesman for humanity at large, embodied and incorporated into the play itself. Herein, he says, lies the poetic significance of the chorus, not to be confounded with its origin, its primitive relation to the worship of Dionysus.[73] Circumstances, then, give rise to a special form that in time comes to be exploited for new reasons.

Part III

The Mind at a Loss: Nonadaptive Thinking

15 *Magic*

The Origin of Magical Beliefs

In general animals pursue what is good for them. Exceptions to adaptive behavior occur when their conditions of life are abruptly changed. The flight of the moth into the flame can be explained by supposing that, before men introduced candles into the world, these insects were led by their instinct to find pale blossoms in the starlight on which they might refresh themselves. The altered circumstances made their useful instinct sometimes suicidal. To explain the existence of such nonadaptive tendencies, we have to look into the past to see under what conditions they could have come into existence with advantage to the animal. Since the conditions of life for the higher animals are complex, and not stable or constant over long periods, present behavior is usually found to be only moderately well adapted. As a consequence we find that desire and pleasure are more or less divorced from physiological usefulness. In the case of man, it is impossible to explain all his tastes and desires on the simple principle that they lead to useful behavior. In many cases they are survivals from a time when he lived in quite different conditions; and while they may have been adapted to his needs at one time in the past, they are sometimes far from being adaptive now. Adaptation is not a law of organic behavior. It is merely a common consequence of those laws. It is the rule; but with humans the exceptions, just because of their tragic importance, loom large, and the near-sighted observer may even overlook the many adaptive tendencies and see only the imperfections and failures.

One of the most startling instances of nonadaptive human behavior is the universal proliferation of magical beliefs and practices. Before discussing this aberration, I must refer again to the subject of abstraction. Without abstraction there could be no learning from experience, for this implies the repetition of the same experience, the same situation. But in reality no situation is exactly repeated, and unless irrelevant differences could be ignored, recognition of a situation would be impossible. It is only to the more extreme cases of such ignoring of differences that the term *abstraction* is usually applied. But there is no important psychological difference between a dog's recognition of the effective situation 'bone', ignoring irrelevant accidents, and a man's recognition of the effective situation 'mammal', 'drug', 'solvent', and so on. In each case situations that are actually different are responded to as if they were the same in virtue of certain common elements which, taken together, constitute the effective situation. Unless these elements are correctly selected, the response will be inappropriate, and the animal is then said to mistake one thing for another.

In man the process of abstraction increases as his range of experience increases, and the possibilities of error and confusion are accordingly multiplied. Moreover, in the complex sequences of human behavior the inappropriateness of a response is not always obvious. Someone who responds to a conflagration by treating it with ether, believing this substance to be a good extinguisher, will indeed experience a rude shock, and if he survives the belief will not survive with him. But he can readily retain for the whole of his life all manner of fantasies concerning matters where the effects of his own actions are less immediate. In such cases he cannot easily devise an alternative method of his own but tends rather to act in the manner he has learned from tradition. If what he does fails in due course to produce the desired result, he may well ascribe the failure to some omission of his own, some error in carrying out the traditional procedure. Out of scrupulous attention to every detail there grew the notion of the special sanctity of tradition. A certain practice, procedure, or ceremonial was known or believed to achieve a particular desired result. Whenever it was repeated, the most fastidious care was exercised to ensure that no detail, however apparently trivial, should be omitted. Ceremonies performed only at long intervals on special occasions would continue to be repeated generation after generation with only the slightest departure from tradition. Much—in some cases all—of the procedure was in reality without effect.

For example, the scattering of seed would be accompanied by many superfluous ceremonies. Ceremonies for the production of rain owed their success solely to the season at which they were performed. On the other hand practices performed daily by ordinary folk—cooking, for instance, or fashioning implements—were abbreviated by haste and carelessness and so gradually pruned of their inessential features. But the condition on which alone this could be successfully achieved was that success or failure should announce itself quickly and unequivocally. When circumstances were favorable to this, useful inventions were made and improved, and the foundations of science were laid. When they were unfavorable, futile and ineffectual practices continued to prevail. It is with the latter that we are concerned at present. I hope to show that magic and science are not, as is commonly supposed, the outcome of separate or opposing mental processes. They are alike in being based on induction; they differ in that most types of magic are based on bad, or merely premature, induction.

When primitive people invent traps and weapons, ploughs and looms, anthropologists do not seek psychological explanations.[74] But when they invent raincharms and bullroarers, anthropologists tend to construct a special psychological theory to account for these aberrations. However, all human behavior, whether adaptive or not, whether savage or civilized, must be accounted for in terms of intelligible general principles of psychology that are universally applicable, not contrived ad hoc for each particular problem.

Many plants are found from experience to yield medicines and poisons. Applied externally or taken internally, they have unmistakable and constant effects, sometimes agreeable and sometimes not. The real connection between the herb and its effects is unknown; but it is a logical process of induction to argue that, since so many plants are found to produce interesting effects on the human body, there is no a priori reason why we should not be able to discover a plant to produce any particular effect we happen to desire. If one can induce sleep by administering a decoction of poppies and by other suitable prescriptions induce vomiting, dreams, intoxication, and even death, why should one not hope to find plants capable of inducing forgetfulness, corporal transformation, the power of prophecy, or the passion of love? It is only from our more exact knowledge of the active principles in plants and their relation to human physiology that we are better able to decide what is possible and what is not. In the absence of such knowledge, the sanguine expectation was not illogical.

In the same way, astrology grew out of authentic observations of a real correlation between celestial and terrestrial phenomena. The positions of the stars are in truth correlated with the changing seasons. The connection between the position of the stars and the significant terrestrial events they portended was as obscure as that between the herb and its medicinal efficacy. But if the stars determined the succession of seasons, why should they not also determine other vital conditions of human prosperity and perhaps man's calamities as well?

Again, alchemy can be traced to bona fide chemical observations. The many observed cases of material transformation (as when metals are extracted from ore), the true conditions of which were unknown, would easily lead to the generalization that suitable manipulation by fire and other agencies could perhaps convert any material into any other.

So again with the various forms of augury and divination: the gods were supposed to communicate their will and pleasure by means of signs, just as men do. Such a belief could be derived only from experience of human communication; it consisted in an extension to all kinds of natural forms and patterns—the intestinal convolutions of animals or the figures produced by flocks of birds in flight—of the signification truly attaching only to the ciphers and characters invented by humans.

A whole class of magical beliefs derives from the primitive gesture-language of self-explanatory signs that must have preceded conventionalized ones. Such magical beliefs consist in an attempt to influence nature by means found efficacious in controlling human beings, namely by gestures. By a movement of the arm one may direct the behavior of a man. We beckon him and he comes, wave him away and he retires. These gestures are so habitual that we make them involuntarily even when they are necessarily ineffectual. We look at a man and he knows that we are thinking of him. The eyes are the focus of every facial expression, and reading a person's face is much the same as reading his eyes. Even animals, when they look at you, look at your eyes, and a facial expression can command obedience as much as a manual gesture or a word. Here we seem to have the grounds for one type of magic, that which relies on bodily movements such as beckoning, pointing, or jumping—as when savages leap high in their ritual dances in order to encourage their crops to grow. In other words, if I want a man to fetch water, I can convey my wishes by performing the gesture myself. Indeed, in the early stages of human language, when it consisted principally of gestures and when the conventional oral languages of today were still to be invented, such a gesture would have been the obvious way to convey the idea. The magical extension of this gesture simply supposes that what is efficacious in influencing the behavior of other human beings can be equally efficacious on crops.

Where a simple gesture or facial expression does not suffice to communicate an idea to another man, recourse can be had to more elaborate pantomime, which may be supplemented by models, drawings, costumes, and other properties. For instance, the idea of inflicting an injury on someone could be conveyed by the gesture of inflicting an injury on his effigy. This amounted to a command or request that someone should go and perform the act, and fulfillment of this command often followed. The magical extension lies in supposing that the gesture in itself is sufficient to call forth the actual injury in due course. If this seems an extravagant generalization, we do well to remember that, even in these days of oral language, when we wish each other a "Happy New Year" or "Many happy returns" or when we mutter "a plague upon him," the thought that mere expression of the wish will help to bring it true is perhaps half-conscious in our minds. In sum: in order to produce certain effects on the behavior of his neighbor, man learned to use certain objects and acts as means of communication. The illegitimate extension consists in applying these methods to nonliving objects or in applying them too generally.

A comparison of magical practices prevailing at different times and places shows that there is a certain correlation between magical ideas and practical inventions. Pictures, gestures, images, and symbols of various kinds were probably all employed before oral communication was established, both for purposes of ordinary communication and for magical ends. Once oral language existed, various magical practices, such as the use of names, could be based on it. In straightforward communication the use of a person's name served to attract his attention, or to make another person think of him. In conjunction with other words, it could result in the named person doing what was required and also (through verbal instructions to other people) in all kinds of things happening to him. The magical use rested on the failure to appreciate the natural limits of such effects. Later the invention of writing brought with it the written charm. Alchemy appeared only after the chemical discoveries involved in metal-working. Mathematical discoveries gave rise to mathematical magic, Pythagorean mysticism, and magical geometrical symbols.

The source of magical ideas may be long forgotten though the resulting practices survive in full vigor. Most men are but little disturbed by the clash of inconsistent ideas. Where problems of an immediate practical nature are concerned, there is a constant weeding out of misconceptions and errors and inadequate notions. But the resulting progress in practical discovery is not incompatible with the survival of many erroneous beliefs less vulnerable to the test of daily experience. The most primitive forms of magic linger today beside the latest scientific advances. The skilled scientist, the enlightened statesman, the boasted skeptic will still be seen at times to treasure a mascot, to partake in a solemn ceremony of magical bread and wine, or pay the immemorial respect to the days of ill-omen. Although magical practices derive from generalizations based on genuine discoveries, they do not become obsolete as soon as there is an advance on the stage of invention in which they originated. Thus the most primitive magical performances based on gestural communication of the pre-oral-language period continue to play their traditional part when oral language has replaced gesture.

Furthermore, old principles are applied to new discoveries: the magical properties attributed to simple herbs can equally well be attributed to modern manufactured drugs whose polysyllabic names and imposing formulas play the part of the mystic inscription on the talisman. Often the same psychological processes are involved. The powers of a particular herb, being poorly understood, were often taken to be much greater than they in fact were. Similarly, today many problems that were formerly difficult to solve can be tackled with a computer; and people who do not understand the real powers of these machines may readily suppose that "asking a computer" will suffice to solve any problem. Such a situation is encouraged because today the gap between the ideas of the more and of the less instructed is far greater than before, since the lowest level remains but little changed. The modern child grows up under conditions that are still in many respects the same as they have been since the beginnings of human society; the important emotional relationships, the routine of physical existence, the psychological adjustments to natural facts and processes, are unaffected except in detail by steel, concrete, petroleum, and electricity. For these additional elements in the modern environment are mostly accepted without being understood, and merely furnish alternative material for religious or magical interpretation. But in modern society there are many grades of intellectual capacity and instruction. The scientists, the inventors, the technicians are, in their own field, far removed in their ideas and mental operations from the ignorant and the incurious. The ideas with which they carry out their thinking are built up out of a vast array of specialized experience and cannot be imparted without such experience to another. But the schools, the press, the universities, and radio and television are continually engaged in the attempt to impart these ideas, and those who listen to the verbal explanations must form ideas to fit them as best they can. Just as in primitive society the less discerning majority gave fanciful interpretations to the doings and sayings of their magicians, so in our society ordinary citizens sometimes assimilate scientific ideas in a form equally fanciful.

When magic was elevated into an art, when it was no longer the common practice but a secret craft, practiced by an exclusive fraternity, new factors were introduced to guide its development. Hocus-pocus began to play a larger part, and this too has its modern equivalent in the form of fantastic inventions, theories, or arguments that claim to achieve, explain, or prove things that they do not and cannot achieve, explain, or prove; consequently, their utility has to be judged on other grounds, such as the hope they offer to the credulous of a short cut around the restrictions of ordinary life, and the prospect to their inventors of power, profit, and prestige. Fundamentally, however, magic of all kinds, ancient and modern, involves the same reasoning process as science. Both rely on observation, generalization, and hypothesis. It is only the more accurate observation, the more careful generalization, and the systematic testing of hypotheses that distinguish science from magic.

Frazer and the Psychology of Magic

As a description of the details of magical practices, the massive work of Sir James Frazer (1854-1941) has a permanent value, which no changes in theory can affect. The Scottish anthropologist's reputation rests firmly upon the sheer exhaustiveness of his encyclopedia of magic, *The Golden Bough.* But on the theoretical side, where psychological questions are involved, he has little to say, and what he has said often seems more akin to that "pseudoscience" of which he himself speaks than to any real interpretation of the phenomena in terms of something that is clearly understood. I quote some examples:

> If we analyze the principles of thought on which magic is based, they will probably be found to resolve themselves into two: first, that like produces like, or that an effect resembles its cause; and second, that things which have once been in contact with each other continue to act on each other at a distance after the physical contact has been severed. The former may be called the Law of Similarity, the latter the Law of Contact or Contagion.[75]

It is not clear what he means by the term *principles of thought.* Are they psychological principles of universal application? In that case all thought must be in accord with the principles, but it manifestly is not. But if such principles of thought are of only limited application, how far does their validity extend? Where do they hold good, and where not? Frazer continues:

> If my analysis of the magician's logic is correct, its two great principles turn out to be merely two different misapplications of the association of ideas. Homoeopathic magic is founded on the association of ideas by similarity: contagious magic is founded on the association of ideas by contiguity. Homoeopathic magic commits the mistake of assuming that things which resemble each other are the same: contagious magic commits the mistake of assuming that things which have once been in contact with each other are always in contact.[76]

Frazer admits that "thus generally stated the two things may be a little difficult to grasp." They are indeed, if we attempt to reconcile them with any known principles of psychology. There is, of course, no evidence that men at any time consistently committed these mistakes. Recorded magical practices lend no support to such a theory. To suppose that the savage who sprinkles water in order to produce rain deludes himself into believing that the water he sprinkles is the rain he desires, that he who makes a waxen image of his enemy confounds the image with the enemy, that the peasants who jump to make their crops grow cannot distinguish between themselves and their crops, that the mariner who whistles for the wind is liable to mistake his own breath for that of Aeolus—to suppose all these things would be somewhat fanciful. "Both trains of thought," says Frazer, "are in fact extremely simple and elementary. It could hardly be otherwise, since they are familiar in the concrete, though certainly not in the abstract, to the crude intelligence not only of the savage, but of ignorant and dull-witted people everywhere."[77]

But it is really not possible to believe that any group of people, however dull-witted, could ever have believed that all similar things were the same thing, and that all things that were ever in contact remain so forever. A race of lunatics holding such beliefs could not have survived for a single generation, even under the most favorable conditions: He adds:

> Both branches of magic, the homoeopathic and the contagious, may conveniently be comprehended under the general name of Sympathetic Magic, since both assume that things act on each other at a distance through a secret sympathy, the impulse being transmitted from one to the other by means of what we may conceive as a kind of invisible ether, not unlike that which is postulated by modern science for a precisely similar purpose.[78]

But if one "law" states that things that resemble one another are the same thing and the other states that things once in contact remain in contact, what need is there for this invisible ether through which impulses may be transmitted? If things are conceived as influencing one another at a distance, it is unnecessary to suppose that they are in contact, still less that they are the same thing. Certainly some magical practices seem to involve the assumption that things may influence one another at a distance (so, for that matter, do many of the experiences of everyday life). Yet the postulate of a "kind of invisible ether" seems to imply the contrary: that man is incapable of conceiving action at a distance and must therefore imagine a medium through which action may be transmitted.

What then are the laws of thought that lead to these fallacies? What are the factors in the natural or the social environment that lead the same type of mind now to science and now to magic? These are the real questions, and Frazer did not answer them because he did not form a clear conception of magic.

The nearest he came to a definition is in the following passage:

> From the earliest times man has been engaged in a search for general rules whereby to turn the order of natural phenomena to his own advantage, and in the long search he has scraped together a great hoard of such maxims, some of them golden and some of them mere dross. The true or golden rules constitute the body of applied science which we call the arts; the false are magic.[79]

This amounts to defining magic as the totality of fallacious generalizations propounded and acted upon in the course of men's search for the laws of nature. It must include all discredited scientific theories that have been made the basis for any kind of practical application. In fact, according to this definition, magic becomes practically synonymous with error. Possibly what is commonly called magic cannot be distinguished by any definite constant character from other forms of fallacy and misconception. But in that case Frazer's illustrations are not representative, and there are many fallacies besides those allowed for in his classification. It appears to me that it is because he failed to take note of several typical and tenacious fallacies that he missed the true generalization. The same psychological factors that gave rise to magic may have been at work in his own case, with the result that he too has given dross instead of gold.

In the background of Frazer's discussion are certain vague principles on which the chief points of the argument are supposed to rest. Chief among these are the "laws of association." He says:

> The fatal flaw of magic lies not in its general assumption of a sequence of events determined by law, but in its total misconception of the nature of the particular laws which govern that sequence. If we analyse the various cases of sympathetic magic . . . we shall find . . . that they are all mistaken applications of one or other of two great fundamental laws of thought . . . The principles of association are excellent in themselves, and indeed absolutely essential to the working of the human mind. Legitimately applied they yield science; illegitimately applied they yield magic, the bastard sister of science.[80]

What then are these two principles that account for so much? And what can be meant by the "application of a fundamental law of thought"? How can a law of thought be either applied or misapplied? If *law of thought* means anything, it must surely mean a constant mode of activity that characterizes the thinking process at all times. Now when we speak of the association of ideas by similarity or contiguity, we give a name to the process by which ideas appear to follow one another spontaneously. The sequence is described in terms of the relation in content of the successive ideas. It is observed that thoughts do not follow one another arbitrarily but are generally bound together by some element they possess in common. This element may consist in a superficial resemblance between the objects represented by the thoughts (association by similarity), or it may be simply the fact that the thoughts have previously occurred in succession as a result of some environmental sequence. This does not exhaust the modes of association, but these are the most familiar in manuals of psychology. The associative process, whatever its physiological basis may be, is a mental characteristic common to animals and man. Frazer seems to assume that two ideas thus associated may become confounded; that is to say, because I associate 'window' with 'door' or 'bath' with 'bun', I may, if I am not cautious, walk through my window or try to eat my bath. I have known dogs to associate 'hat' and 'stick' with 'walk', but never one that could be satisfied by the former in lieu of the latter. Yet Frazer seems to suppose that savages are prone to this kind of thing.

If Frazer's "laws" are truly psychological laws, he would appear to be asserting that it is a necessity of the human mind to believe that "like produces like" and that "things which have been in contact continue to act on each other at a distance." He might perhaps have said that these were not universal principles but principles of *savage* thought. In that case we are compelled to inquire when they became obsolete, and in particular how a mind of such a type could produce the valuable inventions with which we find "savages" acquainted. But it is surely obvious that we are dealing not with psychological laws but with inductive generalizations. The savage thinks he observes action at a distance. Some scientists used to believe that such action does not occur. This is sufficient evidence that neither belief depends on any imperative law of thought.

Frazer distinguishes between religion and magic. But this distinction rests on a modern idea. We are accustomed to the gulf between religion and everyday life. For more primitive people religion is an important part of everyday life and not divorced from it. We distinguish between natural laws and religious truths because we choose to preserve religion while we pursue science. But for primitive man religious truths and scientific laws were all of a piece. Our first problem is to understand the confused state of mind we have got into ourselves. We recognize two independent series of truths, independent yet coexisting. One set commands our attention because of its evident usefulness, the other because it is attractive in itself, flatters our vanity, and calms our fears. Unable to dispense with science yet unwilling to forego hope and consolation, we divide our minds between two mutually exclusive sets of ideas, term one *science* and the other *religion* and proceed to project the distinction into the minds of primitive men. Doubtless primitive men were also sometimes torn between an unwilling recognition of the cruelty of life and an unreasoning belief in its ultimate goodness. But as error was equally mixed with both notions, and as both rested on imperfect and ill-organized observation, it is misleading to make the contrast parallel with that between science and religion. Frazer says:

> If religion involves, first, a belief in superhuman beings who rule the world, and, second, an attempt to win their favour, it clearly assumes that the course of nature is to some extent elastic or variable, and that we can persuade or induce the mighty beings who control it to deflect, for our benefit, the current of events from the channel in which they would otherwise flow. Now this implied elasticity or variability of nature is directly opposed to the principles of magic as well as of science, both of which assume that the processes of nature are rigid and invariable in their operation, and that they can as little be turned from their course by persuasion and entreaty as by threats and intimidation.[81]

When we take into consideration the widespread anthropomorphic views of nature among primitive men, this distinction becomes meaningless. Before the idea of spiritual gods was arrived at, all natural objects—mountains, trees, clouds, rivers, and anything else that attracted attention and was a significant part of the environment—were endowed more or less with human attributes. This merely means that men sought to influence the behavior of other things by the same methods that they found successful in the case of their fellows. Of course the opposite process must also have occurred. Whenever a method of controlling a part of the environment was proved efficacious, it would be extended experimentally to other parts. Anthropomorphism is but one prevalent form of this extension. The two distinct methods of control to which

Frazer refers are merely those found by experience to be efficacious, the one in the case of humans and animals, the other in the case of inanimate things. That confusion occurred is the natural consequence of the inability to distinguish the two categories or appreciate their essential differences. The question posed by Frazer, "Are the forces which govern the world conscious and personal, or unconscious and impersonal?," could hardly have been formulated by savages.

Let me argue this important point more fully. Frazer, in the passage quoted above, is accusing primitive man of inconsistency in that he uttered prayers (which are persuasive) and incantations (spells that bind) in almost the same breath in order to get what he wanted. But that propitiatory and magical methods really are inconsistent is questionable. Both animals and men try to adapt their methods to the differing requirements of different situations. In dealing with inanimate objects, or recalcitrant live ones, we have to use force or mechanical methods, but with voluntary agents we adopt persuasion. Dogs in dealing with men, and men with dogs, use persuasion in general but force on occasion. If we can get a living being to do our will by one means rather than another we choose that means. We learn in time that the method of persuasion or propitiation is not available when we are dealing with stocks and stones. But there is no reason for distinguishing the particular method appropriate for living things from all other methods, since these differ just as much one from another. When a farmer sets up a scarecrow in his fields, or when a cat arches its back and spits at an approaching dog, they are simply using the means at their disposal for dealing with a particular situation. When the dog seeks to persuade his master to take him for a walk he employs various gestures of entreaty. Is this religion or magic? It is obvious that there is no useful psychological distinction between any one method and all the rest. For each animal we have to study the requirements in relation to the environment and the various forms of behavior by which these requirements are met.

Later on Frazer suggests that magic is older than religion; that is to say, the conception of unconscious, impersonal powers is older than that of conscious, personal ones. Yet on the whole human mental development has moved in the opposite direction. Men being the most important ingredient in the environment of man, as soon as he had come to live in communities, the mode of procedure appropriate to this particular element in the environment would tend to be specially developed. Since every new method must be derived from some previously practiced method adapted to the new conditions, it is natural to suppose that the anthropomorphic procedure was more widespread in the early stages than in the later. And so we see, in fact, the scope of the anthropomorphic method gradually contract. One by one the familiar objects of the environment were deprived of their human attributes as specific and efficacious methods of dealing with them were established by experience. Even this did not lead to a dualistic division into animate and inanimate, since the latter class was made up of a multitude of totally different kinds of things, each needing to be treated in a special way. The progress has been from a general anthropomorphism to a specialism that adapted methods to particular situations. New situations could only be dealt with, to begin with, by established methods, and these must always be to some extent inappropriate or inadequate.

Primitive magic, so far from resting, like science, on a clear recognition of the impersonal forces in nature, represents an attempt to influence nature as if it consisted of animate beings. The magician commands the elements by verbal spells. The distinction between prayer and verbal magic is not easily drawn. But what of "sympathetic magic"? The answer I have given in the first section of this chapter is that so-called sympathetic magic is derived from the primitive gesture-language and consists in attempts to influence the anthropomorphically conceived forces of nature by means found efficacious in controlling human beings, namely by gestures. If we assume that there was a time when men had learned to influence one another by means of gestures and the manipulation of symbolic objects, we cannot suppose that they would always understand the nature of the influence they were exerting. All they would understand would be that certain objects and actions, and certain combinations of object and action, did in fact bring about certain results in the behavior of other beings. The extent of such influence not being understood, all kinds of magical practices could result. We do not have to assume any special psychological principle. The so-called savage, in applying his magical psychological methods, was acting on experience, like any other animal, and his more frequent errors were due to the multiplicity and therefore greater ambiguity of his experience.

The reason for the fantastic proliferation of errors in man, as compared with less intelligent animals, is not far to seek. The dog or cat deals appropriately with different parts of his environment. Within a certain limited sphere of familiar objects it acts adequately, scientifically. It can, within this range, do as it will and control its environment confidently and with uniform success. Its powers are very limited by human standards, but its needs are more restricted. Of course, within this sphere, the animal does not treat every object in the same way. It pursues its quarry, or lies in ambush for it, it seeks out shelter, selects a resting place, and consorts with its kind. Its behavior is appropriate to most circumstances and may be regarded as scientific, since it is rationally based on ample experience. But in the animal's dealings with its master the position is different. It cannot control the actions of its master with the same confidence; nevertheless a dog can propitiate him, beg of him, plead with him, and exercise all the religious arts to extract favors from him. We have therefore the same distinction in the behavior of a cat or dog as we have seen in primitive man, and on which Frazer would base the distinction between religion on the one hand and magic or science on the other. In relation to its material environment the dog behaves as if nature were invariable and unconscious, but in relation to its human environment it seems to assume variability and consciousness. The inference which Frazer draws in the case of the savage should be equally applicable in the case of the dog. But though we may admit that the dog has his religion and his science, it is hard to accuse him of practicing magic. We cannot point to any persistent form of reaction definitely aimed at some object it nevertheless fails to achieve. Such behavior is eliminated. It is not that the animal never makes erroneous or ill-advised attempts to gain its ends, but it does not persist indefinitely in such ill-adapted behavior in the same way that men do. The explanation is that magical practices survive only because the bond between action and result is remote enough to prevent the failure of the latter from inhibiting the former. The animal's behavior is aimed at immediate results, and success or failure immediately reacts on behavior.

16 *Theories of Souls and Spirits*

Since the use of theoretical models involves the explanation of novel phenomena by reference to phenomena that are known, it only becomes possible when men have acquired a good deal of experience about the common things and events of their environment. They know, for example, how to mold objects out of mud or clay and how to bind objects together; they are familiar with many of the properties of water, earth, plants, and animals; and above all they know a great many things about the reactions of their own kind—how men may be flattered, cheated, cajoled, frightened, bullied, and, in the last resort, liquidated. They know enough about all these things to be able to predict the course of events and the behavior of objects in a number of possible situations. When with a store of such experience they meet new events or have their attention drawn to new aspects of their environment, they can only try to explain them by analogy with what they already know.

An early type of model that man experimented with was the human model. Nothing in the world seemed better known to him than his own and his fellows' actions and motives, and he naturally sought to explain all phenomena by reference to the one type of behavior he felt he understood. This type of explanation may assume more than one form. A tree may be credited with thoughts and desires like a man, although it manifestly does not have the form of a man. An animal can more easily be equipped with human mental characteristics, since its shape bears some analogy to that of the human body. Storms, rain, rivers, mountains may also be endowed with human faculties, or they may be regarded as the instruments, activities, or dwellings of manlike creatures. This anthropomorphism need not involve any idea of soul or spirit. The phenomena of nature are regarded simply as acting with human motives and human knowledge, not as inhabited by souls capable of existence apart from their habitation. The latter theory could arise only after man had come to regard himself as having a soul distinct from his body. I shall try to show how such ideas originated.

Whereas the human model interprets nonhuman behavior by analogy with human behavior, theories of the soul seek to explain the less understandable parts of human behavior itself. They are contrived to account for life and death, dreams and visions, unconsciousness, sleep and sickness (particularly various symptoms of nervous maladies). The most conspicuous difference between a living body and a dead one consists in the cessation of movement, particularly of heart, pulse, and respiration. Something airy and invisible but not quite intangible seems to escape from the mouth at the moment of death. How was it to be conceived, where was it housed during life, and where does it go at death? To such questions there were many answers, all based on the data of experience, all of them more or less adequate constructive hypotheses.

The problem posed by dreams is that in them one experiences adventures, yet one is assured by one's companions in the tent or room that, during the whole night, one has not gone out on adventures but has remained motionless. The characteristic of a dream, apart from its possible internal incoherence, which need not be conspicuous, is just this complete inconsistency between the experience of the dreamer and that of his companions. Also dreams are sometimes hard to fit into the framework of the waking life. These two factors can be accounted for by the hypothesis of a soul or ghost-self, which can leave the body for a time, roam the country, and then return to its normal corporeal abode. Furthermore, during dreams one meets friends and talks with them, yet thereafter these same friends know nothing of the meeting. Some semblance of them therefore had been separated for a time from their bodily selves without the knowledge of the latter. More striking still, sometimes these simulacra belong to the dead. They must therefore represent some portion of the person that survived the dissipation of death. As a result of these observations, it is not surprising that the living individual was regarded as a complex association of more or less independent elements.

The materials for the construction of the soul as an explanatory model are: the breath, the shadow, the reflection, the echo, and all kinds of vaporous forms that arise and vanish, assuming strange and inconstant forms. Out of these familiar experiences is constructed the airy, intangible, protean spirit, which is supposed to dwell within the living body and, escaping, leave the inert corporeal abode behind. The essential characteristic of bodies or material things is solidity, resistance to the touch. The soul was naturally regarded as immaterial; it might be or become visible, audible, possessed of all the outward characteristics of being, but intangible, unsubstantial, and more or less inaccessible. The materials of such a conception are easily found in shadows and reflections, and occasionally in hallucinations; all these furnish the model of an intangible likeness that can exist separate from the bodily form. Birds and flying insects, which appear to support themselves inexplicably in space, have also been regarded as a kind of incarnation of the spirit that had left its human abode.

Two other obvious points are relevant to the development of soul theories. First, the name of the thing used as the model is often retained in its new application. Thus the soul, if modeled on the breath, was called *breath (pneuma).* But in time, this word ceased to be used in its original sense of 'breath', was replaced for that purpose by a different word, and came to mean only 'soul'. In this manner *pneuma* and other such words (*psyche, anima, spiritus*) came to be regarded as authentic names of real things. Originally the soul was not a real thing, like the heart or liver, but an explanatory hypothesis. But in time it came to be accepted as a real thing, and it then became something as real as the heart or liver, and which needed to be accounted for as they did. In this way it is subtly insinuated that the argument is not about whether the soul exists at all, but only about how to account for its undoubted existence.

This procedure—treating as a phenomenon to be explained what is in fact merely a previously propounded hypothesis—is a frequent source of vain theorizing. Instead of the legitimate attempt to find a hypothesis to explain a set of facts, there is substituted that of seeking the properties of a vague and purely hypothetical entity whose only constant property is its name. The same happens with abstractions. Some of our commonest and most useful words (for example, *knowledge, truth, reality*) are used in innumerable ways, the meaning on any particular occasion depending on the immediate context and the understanding of the persons conversing. But philosophers will take such words as the names of extremely subtle entities and struggle through whole volumes of pseudoanalysis in the ostensible effort to ascertain their hidden nature.

Second, the beliefs of a people are beliefs of a large number of different individuals, who have had different experiences and who are unequally endowed mentally. A more intelligent man may observe things and contrive theories for things that are unobserved or not understood by the majority of his fellows. If he tries to describe what he has seen or thought, he is very likely to be misunderstood. Thus many of the beliefs we meet may be corrupted rather than rudimentary ones, and we cannot assume that every belief recorded can be traced back to an act of rational explanation, at least not directly. The importance of all this is obvious from the fact that most men form theories on the basis of hearsay rather than direct inquiry. The experience of one man, together with his explanation of it, may be accepted by a whole village who have never had the same experience. In Europe, witchcraft must have been believed in by millions who never had any direct experience of its manifestations. If nobody believed in ghosts but those who had actually seen one, the belief would be less widespread than it is. If the listener believes the story, he is apt to be as convinced as though he had been a witness. Soul and ghost theories would have had a different history if men were more skeptical.

How can a fantastic constructive hypothesis be distinguished from one that is adequate as an explanation? It is one thing to attribute an extra large series of footprints to an extra large animal, another to attribute enormous holes in the ground to the feet of a giant. The difference lies in the independent credibility of large animals and giants. Many natural features of the landscape have been attributed to the action of giants. It may be that the phenomena to be explained are such as might well have been produced by beings of a certain size and form, and yet we would not accept the explanation if we did not believe that such beings existed. The explicandum (what it is we are trying to explain) must not only be adequately accounted for by the hypothesis, but the hypothesis must be credible in itself. That is to say, the hypothesis must be consistent with the rest of our knowledge. The French naturalist Georges Cuvier (1769-1832) is said to have claimed that he could infer the habits of an animal from the shape of its skeleton, and within limits a modern comparative anatomist would make a similar claim. But such explanation of anatomical structure by reference to hypothetical habits is reliable only on the basis of considerable knowledge. Animals are a kind of being with which some of us are well acquainted in a very great number of forms, and in consequence we have ample data for generalizing the correlation between variation in form and variation in habit.

The case is rather different when the hypothesis involves imaginary things of a type less well represented in our experiences. This applies particularly to explanations in terms of microstructure, where observed phenomena are supposed to be due to the not directly observable motions and changes of smaller or less accessible entities. The behavior of these entities is always modeled on something familiar in ordinary experience. The atomic theory of Democritus was based on the observation of dust particles and similar phenomena, knowledge of which was very imperfect anyway, so that it was not possible to predict what would happen if very much smaller particles existed, nor to say whether they would in fact produce the familiar appearances of the real world. At a time when the laws of motion were unknown, how could such a model offer any advantages over the phenomena it was designed to explain? The very imperfection of knowledge assisted the construction of such a hypothesis, since it prevented any process of control and criticism. The difference between atomic theories and soul theories is, however, that the former have continually been refined by experiments deliberately contrived to test them.

It is not helpful to explain an observed sequence as the consequence of an invisible sequence if we cannot say exactly what is the relation between the two. The hypothetical machinery must be clearly defined and the laws of its behavior clearly stated. A genuine hypothesis must be verifiable. We must be able to say: If the hypothesis is a good one, we may expect the following things to happen; if they do not happen, the hypothesis is defective and can perhaps be modified. But if we can never make any inference from it, if we do not know what to expect in any particular case, then the hypothesis is merely verbal.

Supposing, for instance, a man is able to know things about our personal history without apparently having had any opportunity of getting the information. He has no known means of coming by his ideas, and so must possess some unknown means. This kind of problem is familiar in every laboratory: a phenomenon is observed to occur, but the reason for it is not known and hypotheses are called for to explain it. In the laboratory no hypothesis is considered of much value if, while explaining the particular phenomenon, it is seen to be incompatible with numerous others, already well known. The scientist's problem consists in finding an explanation for the new observation that harmonizes with all other equally authentic observations. A hypothesis that has no bearing on any other phenomenon would not serve his needs because it could not be tested. In order to test it we must set up the conditions it assumes and observe the result. If we cannot set them up or even recognize them when they are present, then we can never confirm or disprove the hypothesis.

If the man's knowledge is attributed to the promptings of a spirit, then we are assuming the existence not only of an agent not present to our senses but also of one whose powers are unknown. We have no means of knowing when the agent is present, we cannot exercise any regular control over him. We know nothing about spirits and their means of obtaining information and of handing it on to human beings, and so we cannot say in what circumstances this kind of thing will occur and when not. In fact the hypothesis is merely a verbal pseudo-explanation. It has no meaning except that it is the name of the unknown something with unknown powers that is responsible for this particular unexplained occurrence.

Anthropologists have of course collected many examples of beliefs in the transference of such spiritual or abstract things as pain, health, disease, luck, and so forth by means of physical objects. These entities are conceived as beings that can be decoyed away from the victim and removed to a place where they can do no harm, or alternatively summoned from their usual retreat to the person who wishes to benefit from them. The invisible germs of disease are certainly transmitted from one person or thing to another, and the transference of other evils has been explained in the same way. The germ, however (such as the tuberculosis bacillus), can be isolated and experiments can then establish what is fatal to it but harmless to its host. But many people, who have no knowledge of bacteriology, cannot distinguish the transference of germs from the transference of other evils, and if the one is well-founded in experience, then so is the other.

It is only the well-established generalizations of science that enable us to judge what is probable and what is impossible. We know that it is impossible for anyone to set fire to the sea by throwing a match into it. There are some things that would astonish us if we saw them happen, although we are not quite sure that they are impossible. This is because the branches of science concerned with them are not sufficiently far advanced. If we knew as much about psychology as we do about physics, we should regard some of the things alleged about human behavior with extreme skepticism. Unfortunately our psychologists are not very successful in explaining any part of human behavior, so it is hardly surprising that they should have failed to deal adequately with exceptional forms of experience.

17 *Metaphysics: The Problem of Appearance and Reality*

In Chapter 1, I made a distinction between the *real* situation—the actual state of the animal's environment at any moment—and the *sensory* situation, and said that the evolution of behavior depends on a gradual progress toward greater appreciation of the real situation. But as I can know the real world only through my sensations and through my ideas based on them, how can I make any distinction between the real world and the world as I know it? Before considering how British philosophers from John Locke (1632-1704) to our own times have tackled this problem, I must draw attention to an important aspect of it that has often been overlooked.

Our knowledge of human nature is derived partly from study of ourselves and partly from observation of other people. It is because we recognize the general similarity of all men that we are able to combine in one picture the information obtained from both sources. If I study Peter and Paul I find many differences, but they have in common all the so-called human characteristics, and I can compare them directly in order to confirm this. I can observe them under like conditions, subject them to the same tests, compare their actions and expressions, and all my findings will be strictly comparable. Whatever experiment I make on one person I can make on every other, *with one exception.* I cannot study myself in the same manner and on exactly the same terms as I study the rest of humanity. I can submit to the same tests, make similar recordings, and compare results with those obtained from other subjects. But there are irreducible differences that separate my estimate of myself from my estimate of any other being. It is important to understand the nature of these differences, for although their existence has been long realized, in psychological and metaphysical speculation they have not always been properly allowed for. Failure to appreciate both the fact that no man's idea of himself can be superposed for comparison upon his idea of another man—and the consequences of this incompatibility—has resulted in much unfruitful metaphysical speculation.

One of the symptoms (and one of the causes) of the confusion is the frequent practice among philosophers of using the first person when they wish to speak of humanity in general. They say, for example, that *we* experience such and such a feeling, that *we* can or cannot conceive such an idea, that *our* ideas are subject to this or that limitation, or that all the phenomena of the universe are nothing but *our* perceptions; but they overlook the twofold origin of their knowledge and the partial incompatibility of the two sets of data.

Let us briefly review the history of the discussion. Locke noted that objects are known only by the sensations they excite and that all ideas are derived from the elements of sensory experience.[82] Berkeley (1685-1753) took the further step of denying that there is any reality other than ideas.[83] But if it is true that one cannot possibly conceive "how any one corporeal sensible thing should exist otherwise than in a mind," it seems to follow that the universe is no more extensive than our present reckoning of it. Berkeley's answer was simple. That part of the universe which is not part of my ideas, or those of other men, must exist in some other mind. "As sure therefore as the sensible world really exists, so sure is there an infinite, omnipresent Spirit who contains and supports it." So a particular object exists not only when you or I see it or think of it. God sees it and thinks of it all the time.

Hume accepted the reasoning which convinced Berkeley that no existence could be demonstrated outside perception, but he concluded that spirit was as unknown as matter and that the assumption of an infinite spirit was therefore groundless.[84] Not that Hume denied the existence of the world around him. He was concerned to demolish the arguments of those who claimed to prove its existence. If, however, the world is in fact nothing more than the totality of my sensations, then not only my physical environment but all other men and women besides myself are merely sensations in my mind; all my friends and neighbors with whom I imagine myself to be exchanging ideas are but portions of this dreamlike world. But as soon as I take these other people to be as real as myself, I must accept as equally real the common environment by reference to which alone we are able to communicate with one another.

Mill accepted the view of Berkeley and Hume that all that is known of the real world is "given" as sensation.[85] He tried to believe that he could speak as though everything consisted only of sensations, and defined matter as "Permanent Possibility of Sensation." There exist, he said, certain laws that determine the sequence of my sensations, and these laws can be established by empirical methods. Every scientific hypothesis must, he held, be so framed that it states what sensations will be experienced in different conceivable contexts. But in fact we find that the laws of science do not as a rule refer to sensations but deal with facts that may be revealed to different people at different times by a great variety of sensations. The sensations may sometimes vary almost indefinitely, yet the fact remains the same—as when twenty people witness the same event from different points of view.

A. J. Ayer seems to have acquired from Mill the idea that the problem consists in translating common language into the language of sense data. In *Language, Truth and Logic* (1936) he speaks not of "ideas" but of "sense-contents," which he regards as a "neutral" word, that is, a way of describing the external concrete environment without any implications about externality.[86] But in fact the word is no more neutral than *idea,* for it implies the existence of senses that are affected by environmental forces and therefore implies the contrast between mind and matter which Berkeley denied. The notion of a sense organ (eye, ear, or nose) being affected by events in the outside world is obviously derived from everyday experience. And the same experience that reveals the existence of sense organs also reveals the objects that stimulate them. If the reality of the external world is queried, then the sense organs and their relation with the external world must also be queried. It is not consistent to retain constructions deriving from everyday experience and to apply them after having questioned the validity of this experience.

Ayer did recognize a certain difficulty that arises when one speaks of "sense-contents" instead of ideas of things. He wrote:

> The sentence "I am sitting in front of a table" can, in principle, be translated into a sentence which does not mention tables, but only sense-contents. But this does not mean that we can simply substitute a sense-content symbol for the symbol 'table' in the original sentence. If we do this, our new sentence, so far from being equivalent to the old, will be a mere piece of nonsense. To obtain a sentence which is equivalent to the sentence about the table, but refers to sense-contents instead, the whole of the original sentence has to be altered.[87]

What he seems to have in mind is this. When I see a table my sensorium is affected in a certain way; colors, forms, smells, sensations of touch, and so forth assail me, and it is conceivable that I might describe this elaborate pattern and sequence of sensations without mentioning a table at all or any other kind of object. But if I were to undertake to describe the table, if I were to say, for example, "brown generally, darker on lower parts, shape squarish, portions protruding downwards," etc., etc., it would not be possible for me to insert this lengthy description into an ordinary sentence about the table—for instance, to say "I was hoping to pawn the brown generally, darker on lower parts . . . " and so forth. If I once committed myself to this kind of lunacy I should have to stick to it. Of course, Ayer did not venture to give an example of this description in terms of sense-contents, for the good reason that it would be quite impossible. The terms that would have to be used, as those included in the fragment suggested, are all borrowed from the language we have constructed for the normal rational purposes of communication, and would be quite meaningless and useless otherwise. Terms for colors, shapes, smells, and other sensations have all been derived from the names of concrete objects, and even though this origin is forgotten the words have all acquired their meaning in each individual mind through association with concrete objects. Therefore we cannot find any means of describing sense-contents except by the analysis of our notions of concrete things. Experience provides us first with the situation, whole and complex, and only gradually do we learn to separate out the parts, the objects, their qualities, their motions, etc. It is the names of objects that we learn first, not the names of qualities, least of all those most abstract of qualities we call sense data.

Yet it remains true that all my ideas are made up out of sensations and memories of sensations—in highly complex patterns and sequences, but still sensations. It is easy to explain by the principles of association how I learn to interpret them as the signs of various objects and events, provided I am supposed to be already acquainted with those objects and events by some other means. But how do I get to know the dog in order that I may attribute to it the sound of its barking? If I seek to confirm the source of the sound, I can only go and look at the dog or touch it. The colored image and the warm feel of its coat are again only signs like the sound of its voice, and there is in fact no independent notion of the dog to which I can refer them all. I can but refer one to the other. The thing is known to me only as a cluster of complex sensations, any one of which may suggest the others. The barking is not the dog any more than the card is the pack, but the pack is nothing but cards, and my idea of a thing is merely a sheaf of associated memories, each one of which can only go back to some momentary sensation.

Perception, as distinct from sensation, is this ability to recognize a situation or a thing from the observation of a single aspect. My knowledge of the world can only be my interpretation of these sensations and memories. I have reason for supposing that my interpretation is, on the whole, somewhat more adequate than that of my dog, but I cannot be confident that it is not in many respects quite unlike the real world. My conception of the real world is based on experience. When I can predict the sequence of events, when I can say with confidence what will be the consequences of this or that action and find my expectation fulfilled, then I regard this as a sign that in this particular I have got to know what the world is really like. Because, through all my life, I have gradually enlarged the field in which such experiences are possible for me, I feel myself to be making slow progress toward a recognition of the real world—or, in other words, I feel that my conception of the world is being gradually modified in such a way as to correspond more and more to that reality.

The philosopher, impressed by the thought that all his knowledge of the world is composed of his own perceptions, which can only be derived mediately from the world itself, is apt to forget that the very notion of perception is formed from observation of other men who are manifestly affected by an external environment. If he is able to distinguish between a tree and the perception of a tree, it is because he has observed other people's reactions to the tree and seen that they can sometimes be mistaken. He has perhaps seen a man take a tree for an animal, or a mirage for an oasis. It is the palpable errors of Peter and Paul that reveal to me that in their dealings with the world they rely on some internal representation of external things, and I explain to myself their errors by supposing some defect in this representation. My own discovered errors might in the end (even if I were alone in the world) lead me to some theory distinguishing truth from fancy, but the conception of a real external world imperfectly mirrored in the human mind must surely be derived in the main from the contemplation of my fellows.

The distinction between "appearance" and "reality" presupposes an observer making a comparison between his observations and those of another observer. The philosopher who maintains or suspects that the whole world, including all other observers, is mere appearance, is claiming to distinguish something as appearance without having been able to contrast it with any reality, and this is surely impossible. If he says that both the other observers and the outside world are only in his own mind, he might pause here and ask where that idea of 'in' came from. Plainly, it came from considering other people and their erroneous observations. If the "reality" of these other observers has to go (they being "mere ideas" in his mind), then everything else about the mind and its interior will have to go too. There is no sense in speaking of the inside if there is no outside.

Let me press this point with an example. When I observe a stick and a dog, I have an idea of the stick and an idea of the dog. I also see that the dog has an idea of the stick, that is, I have an idea of the dog's idea of the stick. This can be represented diagrammatically, putting the ideas inside the observers:

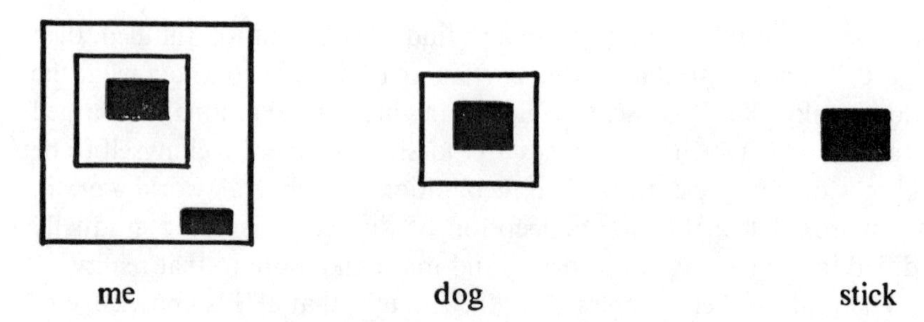

I call my idea of the stick "reality" and the dog's idea of it "appearance," and this distinction presupposes that I can compare and contrast the two. But if I now consider all my observations as a whole, there is no possibility of arriving at this distinction. If it is said that the whole world, as we know it, is illusion, we have not reached this conclusion by contrasting some of our experiences with others. In my own ideas, the bond of association is not between the color, form, feel, or odor of the stick and the "real stick," but between the aforesaid elements themselves. The complex of all these in my mind is, for me, the object, and each of the elements is able to suggest the complex. The "real" object exists for me in contradistinction to someone else's idea of it, not to my own.

In relation to the affairs of ordinary life the distinction between reality and appearance is intelligible enough. At an exhibition of waxworks we are presented with appearance; the figures look like people, whereas they are in reality only bodies carved from blocks of wax. The fisherman's fly appears, I suppose, to the poor fish as an attractive morsel. In reality it is a piece of tin and a feather and worse. The figure that comes to me in my dreams appears to be my father; but in reality it is only a dream. If these are fair samples of the contrast, then it seems that an appearance must always be the appearance of something. And this something which here is counterfeited is assumed to exist somewhere as a reality. A waxwork that resembled neither man nor animal, nor any other known object, could not be called an appearance. We could not say that it "appeared" to be wax, for wax is what it *is*, and the opposition between appearance and reality that is here assumed would vanish. Difficulties arise only when these relative terms—useful for distinguishing one thing from another—are used in an absolute sense, so as to imply that *all that exists* is mere appearance. If the verb instead of the noun were to be used, the same confusion would hardly be possible. If I assert that "the world appears" or "the world seems," it is obvious that the sentence is unfinished and so far meaningless. What does it appear? But when we are told that it is an appearance, the emptiness of the statement is not so evident, so long as we do not stop to reflect what kind of a thing an "appearance" can be. Abstract nouns are more easily swallowed than verbs.

There are, however, cases where the distinction is not so easily drawn, namely apropos of simple qualities like color. The color of an object depends upon the light in which it is seen. The sheet of white paper, under special illumination, appears to be red. That it is in fact white can be shown by exposing it to daylight. That, at least, is the naive view, but on reflection we see that the distinction is arbitrary. Why should the color of the paper seen in sunlight be any more real than that seen in moonlight, or under any other special illumination? Without illumination of some sort we do not see it at all. For practical purposes we accept as normal what is more important or more convenient. But it is only by an arbitrary decision that we can say of the paper that it *is* white but *appears* red, for the whiteness depends as much on the circumstances as any other color. We should therefore say, either that it appears now white and now red, or that it is now one and now the other, and give up the distinction between real and apparent as anything but a matter of convenience.

Thus, where we are dealing with simple characteristics, the distinction is not generally applicable. With complex objects it is otherwise. A bush may look like an animal, a stone like a bird. This is because we usually recognize such objects from a few conspicuous features that may easily prove deceptive. In the distance or in the dark we may mistake a cow for a man because we judge the presence of a man from a vague outline or even a movement. Closer inspection dispels the illusion and reveals the reality. We may say that under special illumination the paper is red, but we do not say that in the dark or in the distance the man is a cow. It seems to be the confusion of these different cases that has helped give rise to the metaphysical notion of appearance. Since the color of a thing depends on all kinds of conditions independent of the thing itself, it seems that we cannot ascribe any "real" color to it at all, and the conclusion is drawn that whatever color we see is mere appearance. A similar argument is applied to shapes. Since the square sheet of paper appears square only if viewed from one particular position, its squareness is held to be only apparent and not real. The English philosopher F. H. Bradley (1846-1924), for instance, would not accept as "real" any quality that is not permanent and independent of conditions. He said:

> A thing must be self-consistent and self-dependent. It either has a quality or has not got it. And if it has it, it can not only have it sometimes, and merely in this or that relation. . . . [88]

These dogmas of "self-consistency" and "self-dependence" that purport to be abstracted from the whole of experience, are in fact an extrapolation ad infinitum. A real dog persists while we examine it; it does not change into a cat on Thursdays or into a teapot in warm weather. If what we took for a dog should evince tendencies of this kind, we should deny its "reality." It is this relative permanence of many material things that is the ground, and the only possible ground, for the precious doctrine that a thing is not real unless it continues the same forever and is unaffected by anything that goes on around it. When "reality" has been thus defined, it is indeed not difficult to show that the world is unreal.

18 *The Quest for Certainty*

I have argued that human thinking differs in complexity but not in kind from the thinking of other animals and that man's science is but a refinement of what a chimpanzee is capable of. Mankind's religion and art are not so obviously paralleled, and attempts have been made to establish them as affording knowledge superior in kind to that of science. The claim has of late been pressed more for art than for religion, which has suffered so many embarrassing defeats at the hands of science, and is made especially, of course, by artists and those who live indirectly on the artist, namely the critic and the literary theorist.

For instance, the American philosopher George Santayana (1863-1952) declared that "the world built up by common sense and natural science is an inadequate world," and "therefore the moment when we realise its inadequacy is the moment when the higher arts find their opportunity. When the world is shattered to bits, they can come and 'build it nearer to the heart's desire.'"[89] The function of art, then, is either to give us the illusion that the world is better than it is or to show that it has certain attractive aspects of which we are ignorant. Now it must surely be the view of Santayana that the world is in fact that better place which art portrays for us and not that worse place depicted by common sense and science. Otherwise art is merely make-believe. So art gives us a deeper insight into the truth of things than science, which, so far from being the only mode of ascertaining the truth about the world, is an inferior mode. Santayana does not ask us to question the findings of science. If they seem incompatible with those of religion and art, this is because there are two kinds of truth, so that "what is false in the science of facts may be true in the science of values."[90] If there is only one kind of knowledge, then we have to bring all our theories into direct relation with one another, contradictions and incoherence being ruled out; but if there are several kinds of knowledge this restriction need not hamper us, and so we may withdraw from the criticism of science any beliefs that its criticism might endanger.

Benedetto Croce (1866–1952) and R. G. Collingwood (1889–1943) are well-known exponents of the view that knowledge based on science, reasoning, and experiment is not the only nor even the most important kind of knowledge. The Italian philosopher Croce argued for "intuitive" knowledge. He held that, as soon as we regard an object scientifically, we cut some of its aspects out of our attention; we "classify" it by means of a "concept," and all classification is relative to some aim. We put different objects into a class in order to emphasize those features they have in common that are important for our purpose.[91] Intuition, on the other hand, does not further our ends nor tell us what objects have in common. It regards an object "in itself" without comparison. Intuitive knowledge is, says Croce, characteristic of the artist. Hence Croce objected to the view "that art is not knowledge, that it does not tell the truth, that it does not belong to the world of theory, but to the world of feeling." He insisted, on the contrary, that "intuition is knowledge, free of concepts."[92] So the artist is not simply telling us what he feels like. He does not give us scientific information, but reveals to us the world as it is, undistorted by concepts or by intellection.

One psychological fact underlying such views is doubtless that an aesthetic attitude to things not usually regarded aesthetically results in an awareness of new aspects of them. A fog at sea, as Edward Bullough pointed out in an influential article, is usually a worrying experience; but if attention is directed "to the features 'objectively' constituting the phenomenon—the veil surrounding you with an opaqueness as of transparent milk, . . . the curious creamy smoothness of the water, hypocritically denying as it were any suggestion of danger," then the experience becomes pleasant.[93] The suggestion is that this change occurs because the object or situation is now seen "objectively," as it really is. But there is in fact still only an appreciation of selected aspects. Many aspects of fog that interest the meteorologist are ignored by the admirer of its "opaque transparency." Nor is it only the aesthetic attitude that makes something take on new aspects. Any change of attitude will have this effect. The fog will appear different according to whether we confront it as a frightened passenger, a painter, a meteorologist, or a sea captain.

Collingwood, a British historian and philosopher, asserted that history, theology, and science are all "special" and "autonomous" forms of thought. He was particularly concerned to establish that history is "its own criterion."[94] Let us consider an example. It is a historical fact that Socrates drank a certain quantity of hemlock and died, and a scientific fact that hemlock contains a poisonous ingredient that can be extracted and administered with lethal effect. The scientific fact is known in much greater detail than the historical one, which is accepted only on the evidence of a few old documents. If the two "facts" were incompatible, most people would agree that it is the historical one that would have to be discarded. Collingwood, however, makes the two classes of fact independent.[95] The context in which he does this suggests that he was swayed by his desire to believe in certain Biblical miracles for which there is a lack of supporting evidence. Clearly, if history has nothing to do with science, then the testimony of the latter cannot be used to impugn the assertions of the former.

The philosopher is apt to think that there must be a superior form of knowledge or reasoning by which one can contemplate the activities of the scientist from outside, from a suprascientific vantage point. The ground for such an exorbitant claim is that the validity of scientific reasoning cannot be established on scientific principles without arguing in a circle, and therefore that if scientific reasoning is valid—as all scientists naturally claim—there must be some extra- or suprascientific process by which science is to be justified; and this, the philosopher maintains, is just philosophy or metaphysics or logical positivism. Many scientists, of course, pursue their investigations without suspecting how unsupported the whole structure of science really is. They do not realize that experimental results prove nothing, that merely because some scientific process has been found to work a million times in industry, in medicine, in the laboratory, there is no philosophic reason at all for supposing that it will ever work again. But there are some more responsible scientists who realize that they have no right to take things for granted in this happy-go-lucky way, and they either accept the authority of the philosopher or assume the role of philosopher themselves. Not uncommonly, they then proceed to argue that the truths of logic, and also of mathematics, are independent of man and his mental idiosyncrasies; that logic is not a permissible subject for psychological inquiry but is directly related to truth; and that, if the principles of logic could be shown to have a psychological explanation, they would cease to be valid. They believe that these principles hold quite independently of the human mind and would remain unaffected even if the universe came to an end.

To this I would reply that the various systems of logic that have been invented were intended as tools for the discovery of truth, or at least for the exclusion of error. Like other tools they are useful for certain purposes, but the way in which they work is not understood and they are commonly credited with powers they do not possess. Man is an animal, and reacts in characteristic ways to his environment. Language, logic, and mathematics are the products of these reactions, just as other forms of science, as well as history, art, religion, and social institutions are products of specific human characteristics in their reaction to the natural and social environment. One must distinguish between natural facts and human reactions to them. The principles of logic and mathematics are based on natural facts, and they are valid just so far as they correspond with these facts. Like maps or charts they are useful guides, provided they have been accurately made. As we have seen, it is sometimes supposed that elementary mathematical truths are not merely more reliable than the facts recorded in the British Pharmacopoeia but reliable in a different sense altogether. According to this view, the chemical and physical properties of cadmium are ascertained by observation and experiment, whereas the multiplication tables are vouched for by our inner consciousness. But if we distinguish between the facts and our methods of formulating them, then in my view the properties of cadmium, whether we are acquainted with them or not, are fixed in the same way and to the same extent as the properties of seven or fifty-three. The conditions for the multiplication tables are incorporated in the structure of the human brain, because it has been highly adapted to the conditions of the universe of which they are a part. The same reasoning applies to all adaptive habits of the brain. Is it not adaptation to the conditions of the real universe that has determined not only our logical habits but also our instinctive fears, repugnances, and desires?

To understand the philosopher, his ideals, ambitions, and illusions, we have to be psychologists. We must know the instinctive human tendencies and the forms of behavior associated with these. We must understand the mind as a mechanism for reasoning and for rationalizing. We cannot claim to understand these things unless we are able to trace the development of the human mental functions from those of simpler animals. We do not know what ideas the trout has of the universe, but we are sure that they are conditioned by its brain. As to whether they are sound, or merely fantasies, we can only say that they enable the fish to survive. That, of course, need not prevent the poor creature from having as many illusions as its betters. We suppose both the trout's brain and our own to have evolved slowly out of the primeval mud. We suppose that each has been adapted gradually to its environment; but we have no guarantee that the brain of any animal can do more than preserve its owner from the more fatal kinds of folly. The tiger's claw and the shark's pectoral fin are efficient for their respective purposes, but not for burrowing or flight. The mammalian brain can guide the animal through the common accidents of its normal environment, but fails before any problem transcending these.

The beliefs, so prevalent among philosophers—that an understanding of first principles must precede sound scientific development, that physical discoveries based on bad mathematics are of no value, that it is more important to have an irrefutable logic than mere experimental ingenuity—are naturally held by those who suppose themselves engaged in the laying of foundations. But the beliefs are erroneous. The so-called first principles of science are in fact the latest and broadest generalizations; one might as well try to build a house from the chimneys downward as to base science on them. Mathematicians spend much time and ingenuity establishing rigorous proofs for methods scientists have found useful. The logician may feel more at ease when this rite has been performed, but its importance to science may be exaggerated. Strictly speaking, there can be no first principles. Any given scientific law may be found to be included, as a special case, in some more general law. Whether this can be accomplished in any particular case depends on whether the knowledge is available and whether an individual mind can be found to comprehend it, so as to conceive the wider formula. As the generalizations become broader, the ideas involved become more abstract and of less immediate practical utility. The so-called first principles of the philosophers and the logicians have lost nearly all intelligible content and seem sometimes to have become mere verbal formulas without utility or interest except to their inventors. It is the concern of the psychologist to explain the whole of this process, from its humble and useful beginnings in practical invention, through the widening generalizations of science, to the final futilities of philosophy.

The problems of metaphysical conundrums seem to arise largely from the failure to recognize the interdependence of all kinds of real knowledge. Physicists have carried their analyses ever further into the realm of the minute, the atom, the electron, and the quantum. Yet it is plain that however far it may be carried, such an analysis must end with the same kind of enigma it set out to solve. However deep one may dig into the constitution of things, one must always pause at some point where fundamental principles come into question. If we succeeded in reducing all observable phenomena to terms of matter and energy or to the mathematical formulas that represent the latter, we should still have to inquire concerning the origin of the ideas with which we are left. We cannot omit to inquire concerning the physicist's mental processes, and the origin of his theories. Such an inquiry can only lead to some kind of psychological interpretation. This, in turn, must lead to the principles of brain physiology, and these back to the principles of chemistry and physics. We have thus returned to our starting point. From this circle there is no escape; but philosophers' dread of "the circular argument" has perhaps prevented appreciation of this.

The whole system of human knowledge is closed. It is not possible to find any small set of fundamental principles on which the whole of science and philosophy can be built. I do not mean merely that they have not been found or that, in view of the difficulties, they are never likely to be found, but rather that there is really no sense in looking for them. Science and philosophy are products of the human mind. A theory of truth is, after all, a theory, that is to say, some kind of human notion based upon some kind of experience and cogitation, a product of the working brain. The brain of man is a product of evolutionary adaptation and, from the physiologist's point of view, only a little superior to that of the ape or the dog. Can any absolute validity be assigned to the ideas it generates? If, as many philosophers hold, the mind is not limited by the relativities of evolution and possesses an access to reality independent of the rational and experimental procedure of science, then what criterion remains by which we may distinguish the wisdom of the philosopher from the delusions of the insane? It seems we must either give up hope of reaching any truth that is not relative or, if we believe ourselves capable of attaining absolute truth, be resigned to never knowing when we have found it. The kind of truth that is based on scientific experiment and hypothesis may fall far short of the ideal of the philosopher; yet the kind that is out of all relation to them must be without practical application.

If all our knowledge is only relative, if there is no proposition whose truth is not conditional on the truth of another, how can we be satisfied about the truth of any? Must we abandon the hope of achieving real knowledge? Not if we remember that many forms of scientific knowledge have made progress despite very meager metaphysical foundations, and their progress has often led to the revision of those "foundations." The so-called fundamental ideas of any science are, after all, only relatively fundamental and are subject to alteration. Biology is based on a number of ideas that, in relation to science as a whole, are not in the least fundamental, are not even clear and generally accepted. They are a temporary makeshift. But this insecure basis is no great disadvantage, and biology has progressed in spite of it. Each branch of science requires some set of elementary ideas to work with, and it revises them as occasion demands. Moreover, one branch will often be in a position to furnish suitable elements with which another can build. Mathematics has thus provided notions to replace the provisional atoms and forces of physics. Physics in turn has supplied chemistry with more adaptable atoms, and chemistry has performed a similar service for biology. We may hope that in due course psychology may be provided with some useful building materials by physiology. Continuing the same process, psychology will at length repay its debt by furnishing the much-needed foundation for philosophy and mathematics. The circle will then be complete. We will no longer try to balance knowledge like an inverted pyramid on some one indisputable yet inconceivable principle, but will let it form a self-supporting system, resting on nothing, owing its coherence and solidarity to internal forces, not susceptible of infinite extension, but finite and exhaustible.

Whether such a view will seem to the reader agreeable or comforting I do not know; but at least, if the aim of philosophy is a truly satisfying answer to all questions, then such a structure of knowledge alone offers any prospect of achieving it. So long as we see the progress of knowledge as a sequence of ever-broadening but less-numerous generalizations, we must expect to come at last to one all-embracing law. But we could not rest content with that and would ask the reason for such a law. If, however, the realm of knowledge has no ultimate and unsupported foundation, if each part is held in place by its cohesion with the rest, then there may at last remain no unanswered question, and no principle not perfectly derived. In the words of Parmenides:

ξυνὸν δέ μοί ἐστιν
ὁππόθεν ἄρξωμαι, τόθι γὰρ πάλιν ἵξομαι αὖθις.

(It is all one to me where I start, because that is where I shall end up).

Notes

1. Dugald Stewart, *Elements of the Philosophy of the Human Mind* (London, 1814), vol. 2, p. 2.

2. Herbert S. Jennings, *Behavior of the Lower Organisms* (New York, 1906).

3. G. S. Fraenkel and D. L. Gunn, *The Orientation of Animals* (Oxford, 1940), p. 136.

4. E. L. Thorndike, *Animal Intelligence* (New York, 1911).

5. Ernst Mach, *Erkenntnis und Irrtum,* 5th ed. (Leipzig, 1926), p. 186.

6. Eugenio Rignano, *La Psychologie du Raisonnement* (Paris, 1920), p. 100.

7. Ibid., p. 101.

8. Wolfgang Köhler, *Intelligenzprüfungen an Menschenaffen,* 2nd ed. (Berlin, 1921); Eng. trans. Ella Winter, 2nd ed. (London, 1927).

9. Ibid. (German ed.), p. 74.

10. Ibid., p. 77.

11. V. Bechterew, *General Principles of Human Reflexology* (1928); trans. E. and W. Murphy (London, 1933), from the Russian of the 4th (1928) ed.

12. J. B. Watson, *Psychology from the Standpoint of a Behaviorist* (Philadelphia and London, 1919).

13. Gilbert Ryle, *The Concept of Mind* (London, 1949), p. 25.

14. In the *Principia* Newton declared: *Hypotheses non fingo* (I invent no hypotheses). In a letter of 1672 he explained that his objection was to hypotheses that "attempt to predetermine the properties of things" instead of first establishing them by experiment and then seeking hypotheses to explain them.

15. I. P. Pavlov, *Conditioned Reflexes,* trans. G. V. Anrep (Oxford, 1927).

16. Erasmus Darwin, *Zoonomia* (Dublin, 1800; first published 1794-1796), vol. 1, p. 137.

17. Aristotle, *De Anima,* trans. E. Wallace (Cambridge, 1882).

18. Henry Havelock Ellis, *Studies in the Psychology of Sex* (London, 1898), vol. 1.

19. Herbert Silberer wrote a number of articles on dreams, 1909-1912.

20. Sigmund Freud, *Die Traumdeutung,* 5th ed. (Leipzig, 1919), p. 236.

21. Ibid.

22. Conway Lloyd Morgan, *Animal Behaviour,* 2nd ed. (London, 1908).

23. Frédéric Paulhan, *The Laws of Feeling,* trans. C. K. Ogden (London, 1930).

24. Herbert Spencer, *The Principles of Psychology,* 4th ed. (London, 1899), vol. 1, p. 108.

25. Neuropsychology, the science that endeavors to relate behavior (including mental behavior) to the anatomy and physiology of the nervous system, is a rapidly evolving discipline. Much has been learned since Englefield wrote. For nonspecialist readers with broad philosophical interests who wish more information on the current state of knowledge, there is Colin Blakemore's *Mechanics of the Mind* (Cambridge, 1977).

26. The following account supplements the cursory treatment of the subject in Chapter 1 of Englefield's *Language: Its Origin and Its Relation to Thought* (London, 1977), hereafter referred to as *Language.*

27. Englefield dealt with imitation in Chapter 4 of *Language.*

28. Köhler, *Intelligenzprüfungen,* p. 92 (see note 8).

29. The use of models in communication and for magical purposes is discussed in *Language,* Chapters 7 and 11.

30. *Language,* Chapter 5.
31. Thomas H. Heath, *Manual of Greek Mathematics* (Oxford, 1931), p. 98.
32. Dugald Stewart, *Elements of the Philosophy of the Human Mind,* vol. 2, p. 206 (see note 1).
33. Alfred Jules Ayer, *Language, Truth and Logic* (London, 1936: 8th printing, 1951), p. 58.
34. Ibid., p. 84.
35. E. B. Tylor, *Primitive Culture,* 3rd ed. (London, 1891), vol. 1, p. 252. Tylor refers to W. von Humboldt's book on the ancient Kawi language of Java *(Über die Kawisprache),* published in 1836, a year after his death.
36. Ibid., pp. 243-44.
37. Ibid., p. 258.
38. F. du Pré Thornton and R. A. Nicholson, *Elementary Arabic* (Cambridge, 1919), p. 17.
39. *Language,* Chapter 7.
40. Ernst Mach, *Die Prinzipien der Wärmelehre,* 4th ed. (Leipzig, 1923), p. 398.
41. Gaston Maspero, *The Dawn of Civilization,* trans. M. L. McClure and ed. A. H. Sayce, 4th ed. (London, 1916), p. 16.
42. Hermann von Helmholtz, *Vorträge und Reden* (Brunswick, 1884), vol. 1, p. 65.
43. Lucretius included an atomic theory in his *De rerum natura.* He was a disciple of the Greek philosopher Epicurus (342-270 B.C.).
44. For details of early atomic theories, see Joshua C. Gregory, *A Short History of Atomism* (London, 1931).
45. Wilhelm Ostwald, *Grundriss der allgemeinen Chemie,* 6th ed. (Dresden and Leipzig, 1920), p. 127.
46. Mach, *Die Prinzipien,* p. 399 (see note 40).
47. Ibid., p. 401.
48. Ibid., p. 402.
49. John Stuart Mill, *A System of Logic,* 5th ed. (London, 1862), vol. 1, pp. 332-34.
50. René Descartes (*Principia Philosophiae,* 1644) suggested that the planets might be impelled by a very fine kind of matter that rotated like a vortex or whirlpool around the sun.
51. Spencer, *Principles of Psychology,* Part 9, Chapter 9 (see note 24).
52. Ibid.
53. Karl Groos, *The Play of Animals,* Eng. trans. (London, 1900), pp. 75-76; reprinted in *Play: Its Role in Development and Evolution,* ed. J. S. Bruner et al. (Penguin Books, 1976), pp. 65-67.
54. Ibid. (1900 ed.), p. 290.
55. Lloyd Morgan, *Animal Behaviour,* p. 254 (see note 22).
56. Ibid.
57. Thorndike, *Animal Intelligence,* p. 244 (see note 4).
58. Alexander Bain, *The Emotions and the Will,* 4th ed. (London, 1899), p. 310.
59. William James, *The Principles of Psychology* (London, 1901), vol. 2, p. 487.
60. Bain, *Emotions and the Will,* p. 310.
61. Ibid., pp. 310-11.
62. James, *Principles of Psychology,* p. 430.
63. David Hume, *A Treatise of Human Nature,* (1739), Book 2, Part 3, Section 10; the quotation is from the Everyman ed., vol. 2, p. 157.
64. A year after Englefield's death, Penguin Books published a volume of essays on play (see note 53). The editors indicate in the Introduction (p. 15) that "one function of play is the opportunity for assembling and reassembling behavior sequences

for skilled action." One editor, J. S. Bruner (in his paper "Nature and Use of Immaturity"), cites Jane von Lawick-Goodall's reference to chimpanzee play with twigs and other objects as possibly being "of tremendous importance in developing dexterity in manipulating objects" (p. 39). Bruner makes "the rather unorthodox suggestion that, in order for tool using to develop, it was essential to have a long period of optional, pressure-free opportunity for combinatorial activity" (p. 38). That he calls this idea unorthodox shows that Englefield's view of play, as argued in this chapter, is far from generally accepted. For another survey of the subject, see the essays in *Play as Exploratory Learning*, ed. Mary Reilly (Beverley Hills, Calif., 1974).

65. See Englefield's *Language* (see note 26).

66. For a fuller treatment of this topic than that which follows, see Englefield's article "The Origin, Functions and Development of Poetry," *Trivium* 10 (1975): 62-73. Some of that material is used in the present volume by kind permission of the editor.

67. Professor Denys Page notes that Greek epic poetry is oral, by which he means "composed in the mind without the help of writing," and that it was "preserved by memory and handed down by word of mouth." "This kind of poetry," he adds, "can only be composed and . . . preserved if the poet has at his disposal a ready-made stock of traditional phrases." The Homeric poems are composed of sequences of such phrases: "In 28,000 lines there are 25,000 repeated phrases, large or small." Page, "The Homeric World," in *The Greeks*, ed. H. Lloyd-Jones (London, 1962), p. 9.

68. Gilbert Murray, *The Classical Tradition in Poetry* (Oxford, 1927), p. 87.

69. J. W. Draper gives evidence that "rhyme in Chinese and related folklores may—and probably does—go back for uncounted centuries." "The Origin of Rhyme," *Revue de littérature comparée* 31 (1957): 31.

70. Murray, *The Classical Tradition in Poetry*, p. 139.

71. W. G. Aston, *History of Japanese Literature* (London, 1899), p. 31.

72. Murray, *The Classical Tradition in Poetry*, p. 124.

73. A. W. Schlegel, *Vorlesungen über dramatische Kunst und Literatur*, Lecture 5 (1808).

74. The following account draws to some extent on Englefield's *Language*, Chapter 11.

75. James George Frazer, *The Golden Bough*, 2nd ed. (London, 1911), vol. 1, p. 52.

76. Ibid., p. 53.

77. Ibid., p. 54.

78. Ibid.

79. Ibid., p. 222.

80. Ibid., pp. 221-2.

81. Ibid., p. 224.

82. John Locke, *Essay Concerning Human Understanding* (1690).

83. George Berkeley, *Dialogues in Opposition to Sceptics and Atheists*, Dialogue 2 (1713).

84. Hume, *A Treatise of Human Nature* (see note 63).

85. Mill, *Examination of Sir William Hamilton's Philosophy* (1865).

86. Ayer, see note 33.

87. Ibid., p. 64.

88. F. H. Bradley, *Appearance and Reality* (London, 1893), Introduction.

89. George Santayana, *Interpretations of Poetry and Religion* (London, 1900), p. 269.

90. Ibid., p. 91.

91. Benedetto Croce, *History as the Story of Liberty*, trans. Sylvia Sprigge (London, 1941), p. 294.

92. Croce, *Aesthetics as Science of Expression and General Linguistic*, trans. D. Ainslie (London, 1909), p. 29.

93. Edward Bullough, "'Psychical Distance' as a Factor in Art and an Aesthetic Principle," *British Journal of Psychology* 5 (1912): 89.

94. R. G. Collingwood, *The Idea of History* (Oxford, 1946), pp. 7, 140.

95. Ibid., p. 136.

Index